Jenny Packham graduated from Saint Martin's School of Art and launched her eponymous fashion label in 1988. Now with stores across the world, she is famed for her beautiful bridal gowns as well as her bespoke dresses for public figures including the Duchess of Cambridge, Adele and Dita Von Teese. She is based in London, and *How to Make a Dress* is her first book.

HOW TO MAKE A DRESS

JENNY PACKHAM

EBURY
PRESS

1

Ebury Press, an imprint of Ebury Publishing,
20 Vauxhall Bridge Road,
London SW1V 2SA

Ebury Press is part of the Penguin Random House group of companies
whose addresses can be found at global.penguinrandomhouse.com

First published by Ebury Press in 2021
This edition published by Ebury Press in 2022

www.penguin.co.uk

A CIP catalogue record for this book is available from the British Library

ISBN 9781529103038

Printed and bound in Great Britain by Clays Ltd, Elcograf S.p.A.

The authorised representative in the EEA is Penguin Random House Ireland,
Morrison Chambers, 32 Nassau Street, Dublin D02 YH68

Penguin Random House is committed to a sustainable future
for our business, our readers and our planet. This book is made
from Forest Stewardship Council® certified paper.

For Mathew

I've been thinking about becoming a 'virtual' designer. I could work without fabric and sewing machines and superimpose my designs onto your image, ready to wear on social media. I will render the fabrics to fit your body, manipulating the colours and giving brilliance to the embellishment with a swipe of my finger. You won't even be able to tell the difference and, after a while, the very notion that your dress isn't real will fade and, maybe, you will almost 'remember' what it felt like to wear your look.

Imagine. With modern technology I could transpose the luminescent wings of a rare butterfly onto the surface of your gown, sending your friends into a flutter; or if you prefer, I could plant hollyhocks and sweet peas around the hem and watch in wonder as they begin to grow and entwine, edging their way up the dress, trailing off your shoulders in delicate disarray.

After all, material excess has had its day, and with my new-found digital craftmanship I will squash my carbon footprint and help to conserve our fragile ecosystem. The fashion industry and its compulsion for seasonal presentations to satiate our desire for constant consumption is now unsustainable. So rather than start counting my sequins and cutting my cloth to reduce the impact of my collections on the environment, I can escape to make eco-fashion, dresses that don't exist, and then with a tap of my finger transport my ideas into hyperspace, before they fall into your pocket with a ping and I count your 'likes' with guilt-free gratification.

Pause. I can't do this. Already I can feel myself slipping away from the joy of being liberated from the treadwheel of fashion. Limitations have been the fuel for my imagination and to create dreams out of challenges has been part of my work. If I were to engage in unbounded creativity I may just implode. Even the choices I will make to help save our planet will force enlightened innovation. Paintings need frames.

Nostalgia for my art has already kicked in and I know that I will miss the trick of cutting on the bias to create a subtler silhouette, and that my fingers will ache for the touch of slipper satin. For years I have held the components of my work in my hands and often inadvertently taken them home, waking up to find crystals and pins lying beside me in bed. These tools and textures, integral to the making of a dress, are as inseparable from me as they are from each other. From inspiration to sketch, pattern to fabric, the making of a dress has been the structure that has held me, and my passion to dress others is the momentum of my life.

This *is* a book about fashion, but mostly it is a book about love.

INSPIRATION

'You can't wait for inspiration. You have to go
after it with a club.' *Jack London*

'Where do you get your inspiration from?'

As the journalist sits down in my studio and pushes play
on her Dictaphone, I know that this will be the first question she will ask. Today I am showing her an edit of dresses
from the last 30 years of my fashion label for an article to
celebrate this milestone. I have chosen my favourite designs
and they are hanging on a rail, forming a glorious jumble of
colours and textures.

I presume that she will ask me about the inspiration for
particular styles, and my answers will be mostly accurate.
However, sometimes I am forced to lie a little, because the
truth behind the creative journey is not always as glamorous
as others anticipate. My intention is to inspire people with

my own inspiration – and, like many artists, I am some-times better at creating than describing my work.

The journalist reaches forward and pulls out the tulle skirt of a dress, holding the fabric and looking closely at the embellishment, and asks me where the pattern for the beadwork originated. I pause, and allow myself to sink back into my memories.

On a family holiday to Scotland, we found ourselves walking around Fort William in the rain and the kids were bored. So we took shelter in the town's museum, where we discovered the usual haphazard collection of chipped pots, Jacobite tableware and crofters' furniture. In the dusty basement a group of headless dummies were gathered wearing various examples of Victorian clothing, and my eye was drawn to a dress with a swarm of iridescent beetle wings sewn on the skirt. They were not fancy beetles, just common Jewels about 3 centimetres long. In a tea room afterwards, I found myself scribbling a dress in my sketch-book – smoky grey chiffon dipped in charcoal dye at the hem, beaded with small green sequins. I called the dress 'Joy'.

I don't tell the journalist this: it is far too ordinary some-how; but I enjoy the family memory and mention to her that the dress was later recoloured into ivory, becoming one of our best-selling bridal gowns. I glance along the rail to a sequinned one-shouldered dress and, while she pauses to write some notes, I readjust the hanging loops so it falls less awkwardly, and my mind travels back to 2005.

A designer I worked with at that time had always told me she had a phobia of moths. One day while opening a box of dresses sent from China, a large-winged one flew out and I realised, as she turned ashen-faced, that it was not a joke, or even just a mild fear, but sheer terror. After that, it was best not to mention them. Eventually she left to live in Japan for a few years, and I missed her terribly. Meanwhile, my new designer found a book of photographed moths in the bookshop beneath my studio. The images were beautiful. Shown in minute detail, the texture and patterning of the moths' wings were irresistible and somehow being inspired by these previously forbidden insects helped me move on from her departure.

This is far too abstract an answer for the journalist, so I mention the moths briefly and show her an effect we created using textured sequins with a velvety finish to imitate their wings. She then lifts from the rail a partly pleated chiffon ballgown that ombrés from white at the hem to light lime green on the bodice, with pretty little lace sleeves.

'So tell me about the collection this one came from. What was the inspiration?'

I imagine that I look vacant for a moment.

After my mum died, I used to sit on Hampstead Heath watching the clouds. It was incredible to me that she would never again see the sky. One day a rainbow appeared, and it seemed totally wondrous in comparison to my colourless grief; and in that moment an idea took root. My next spring/summer collection was 35 looks; the show began with a red dress and travelled the full colour spectrum, gently mutating into white for the final look. The collection was badly received. I don't think it did the rainbow justice.

I keep my sad thoughts to myself and explain how I created the collection by blending colours into one another, gently shading each style to create a rainbow effect running throughout the garments, and then I divert her attention to a short blush-coloured dress.

'I took the idea for this dress from a vintage piece I saw swinging from the metal frame of a Parisian flea market stall,' I say. A pretty mint costume with a strappy satin camisole, studded with little crystals and sewn onto a shortish swing skirt trimmed with wilted ostrich feathers. A dressing-up box dream! It must have caught my eye because I had just read Colin Thubron's novel *Falling*, a tragic story of a doomed love affair involving a high-wire trapeze artist who falls to her death.

'I re-dressed the little heroine in blush and she lived again, strutting her way down a London catwalk,' I say, happy that at last I have been able to answer with conviction.

The journalist seems pleased with the interview. She enquires about my next collection.

'I haven't started it yet. I'm exploring a few ideas,' I say unconvincingly. Then, after she leaves, I take a moment to look at the rail of archive styles. My secrets are intact. I know these stories fall short of being good copy, but the styles inspired by my personal experiences add richness to the rail and are undoubtedly my favourites.

There is something rewarding about finding inspiration in unexpected places.

Sometimes, when I find myself somewhere dull – a motorway service station or a corporate boardroom, for example – I challenge myself to be inspired. This can be an act of escapism, or a way of justifying spending my time somewhere I would rather not be. Queuing in the JFK customs hall after a long flight, I study those ahead of me, analysing and reimagining the fabrication of their clothes; checks and corduroy, prints and colours. It concentrates my mind and, occasionally, there is a spark of inspiration.

*

It is the hottest day in June so far and I am about to catch the bus from South End Green to the British Library. Outside the local newsagent is a vending machine crammed with 'magic squishy balls' for 50p each, every one small and uniquely patterned. These bouncing balls come in many colours: dayglo orange with a hazy swirl of pop-art pink, marbled geranium and primrose yellow, and a Mediterranean cocktail of turquoise and blue dotted with lime. Their hues could easily be thrown together to create a summer palette. My favourite, of course, is the clear one with the suspended flecks of golden glitter.

A queue is forming, and the warm weather has brought out a tropical theme in the crowd. An elderly lady wearing a cerise-coloured wool cardigan stands next to a runner in a sweaty purple T-shirt and cobalt blue cap. Nearby is one of my favourite Hampstead residents – I call him Khaki Man – who is sporting an elderly gentleman's version of shabby chic, including socks with sandals. I mentally scroll through the colours, adding them to my bus stop inspiration file.

Across the road, the White Horse is closed. The former gastropub stands abandoned, its windows encased in gleaming metal. As the morning rays collide with their surface, the passing traffic forms ghostly shadows of greyish-blue, projecting beautiful urban landscapes that might have been painted by Gerhard Richter.

I am lost for a moment, dreaming up a dress of overlapping steely sequins in muted shades, gradually changing tones and sending fiery sparks across a dance floor like a rotating disco ball. The bus arrives, abruptly ending my reverie.

As the bus heads towards town, the pretty front doors of north London's Victorian terraces flit past like a Farrow and Ball colour card, contrasting with the early morning parade of cyclists, their fashionable gear featuring innovative fibres and reflective strips, prompting new design ideas with a sportswear influence: perhaps I could add punch to a classic evening dress with a dash of hyper-dazzle trim?

At Mornington Crescent, as we pull into a stop I see an advertisement for the Tower of London. On it, the face of Anne Boleyn is framed by her familiar French hood, and her pearl-trimmed square neckline jolts me back to my first cinema experience as a child.

Anne of the Thousand Days was a 1969 British costume drama starring Richard Burton and Geneviève Bujold, and for me a matinee moment that ignited a lifelong passion. As the blade fell on Anne, I dropped my popcorn on the floor in surprise and felt pleased the film must be nearly at an end – I wanted to get home and dress up. The film won an Academy Award for Best Costume Design for Margaret Furse. However, Bujold's smooth and seamless corsets, with peeping kirtles that intrigued Henry, were a 1960s spin on sixteenth-century court wear, as implausible as Anne's love. Regardless, the king and I succumbed to her sartorial elegance and sparkling beauty, which lured us both into an obsessive lust.

If picking up inspiration from the streets of north London can be compared to a takeaway, then a visit to the Prado Museum in Madrid is a Michelin-starred tasting menu.

Female portraits in the art galleries of the world are often glamorised. The elegant and rich held still for their artists in return for immortality. Colour, texture and adornment are all used to capture their beauty and spirit – and to convey an image of perfection. These are the paintings that captivated me on my first visit to the Prado some time ago. The gilt-edged women with pearl drop earrings in painterly effects of taffetas, wrapped with rich velvet ribbons like precious gifts. I careered down the palatial corridors like a bee collecting pollen, buzzing between Rubens' three voluptuous Graces and Goya's notoriously naked Maja and coming to rest in a small gallery almost entirely dedicated to Raimundo de Madrazo y Garreta, who, like our own John William Waterhouse, had an eye for beauty and sartorial style. A successful portrait artist, he spent most of his working life in Paris during the mid- to late 1800s, commissioned by the elite to smooth their features and style them into glamorous Annie Leibovitz-like compositions.

Madrazo's paintings portray lusciously coquettish models dressed in spring-like shades of pistachio and strawberry, melting together on the canvas like ice cream. The editorial fashion pages of the nineteenth century, featuring the latest in belle époque couture, were ripe for reinterpretation. The fluid brushstrokes of Raimundo's washes and the museum's collection of Velázquez's baroque 'cut out and fold' dresses juxtaposed themselves in my mind to create visions of structural bodices swathed in soft drapes of flimsy silk.

The ensuing collection was full of courtly decadence and rich vibrancy. Decorative russet-coloured blouses were embroidered with pearls and crystals in the style of matadorial brocades. Crispy lapis lazuli organza ankle-length skirts were belted with velvet bands and styled with transparent shirts. The collection shimmered with molten metallic halter-necked jersey dresses, and plumes of ostrich feathers swirled around peacock sequins on chiffon capes.

Ladies of the Prado – I salute you.

Some time later, on a chilly winter morning, I am standing on the stage of St Stephen's church in Hampstead. The sunlight is piercing the stained-glass windows, throwing haphazard shards of colour across the Mighty Church, as it was once nicknamed on account of its hilltop location and brimming assembly. I lean against a pillar and survey the scene. Today, this part of the church is bereft of pews. Instead, lightbulbs and bunting are draped from pillar to pillar, mocking the Gothic sincerity of the architecture. Below me, a pop-up vintage fair is in full swing. The room smells of mothballs. I'm excited.

There are about 50 racks of clothing, and as many trestle tables. Each rail is packed with hangers, flat plastic or metal for maximum use of space. I scan the room from the second-hand fur in one corner to the rather startling reconstruction of my mum's kitchen circa 1973 in the other. I am drawn to the chocolate-coloured poppy placemats, and for a moment can almost taste the banana-flavoured Angel Delight. And then I flick the switch on my Tupperware daydreams and focus on today's congregation.

In a small second-hand shop on the Portobello Road a decade earlier, I had a moment of creative awakening. As usual, blouses and dresses were crammed in among untidy racks of shoes, gentlemen's ties flopped over hangers, and felt hats, piled too high to reach, surrounded me. It was a woven cave, dusty and seductive.

I'd never thought much about old clothing, but on this day every shoulder pad I touched, every piece of fabric that I pushed aside, felt different. The room was ablaze with memories. A lavender embroidered chiffon dress, rotten and held together only by the threads that secured the beads, seemed to disintegrate beneath my fingers. But I could imagine the thrill of the evening: the show and tell, the giggly twirl, the door slamming behind the girl as she tripped lightly down the porch steps to the waiting car, and then away into the evening. Now, empty threads hung among the fringe of beaded tassels attached at the hip. Perhaps as she danced amid the music and laughter with joyful abandonment, a string snapped, throwing beads across the ballroom floor.

Elsewhere, a shoe peeked out from beneath the skirt hems, a tan court with the leather bulging around where a bunion might have been. Above it was hanging a pretty printed floral blouse from the fifties, perhaps worn on honeymoon in the West Country, and I imagined ice cream drops falling onto the collar as the new bride threw her head back to catch the summer sun.

Huddled at the end of the rail was a collection of funereal Victorian jackets, all black, with hand-stitched corded flowers. These bolero-style jackets with tight underarm seams would only fit a child nowadays and so they will stay grieving for a while longer. In contrast, a sweet hippy 'first kiss' cheesecloth blouse hung from the ceiling ready for another summer of love.

This small room was alive with women chatting and laughing, even dancing, all begging me for acknowledgement. This was a catacomb of women's lives to inspire me.

For years I had forbidden myself to 'copy' others, preferring to think in my youthful arrogance that my ideas would always be my own. But suddenly, recycling the past – connecting with fantasy moments and from them creating something that lived again – seemed a magical prospect. Ever since that day, I have been inspired by vintage clothes – it's like having my own fashion wormhole.

Back in the church, my eyes drift over the table covered in chequered cloth to a squashed satin duchess evening bag, the original price tag still on it. Lying beside the bag is a golden powder compact etched with white lilies and trailing leaves. I hold it, debating whether the pattern would translate onto the bodice of a bridal dress. Compacts are attractive purchases, abundant at such events. As I open it, a small cloud of tinted dusting escapes.

As the musty scent of old talc settles in the air, my imagination presses play on a clichéd girl and boy scenario: a handsome young man pulls up the final notch on his zipper and moves the Alfa's car seat forward from its post-passion position, while a girl swipes the powder across her T-zone before snapping the compact shut, deciding to discard it for a prettier version. Meanwhile, he is thinking the same thing.

I carry on with the smutty theme as I touch a scratchy gold lamé shift dress with a torn split at the side seam, the thin ribbons of metallic fibre broken and twisted. I could imagine this as a Christmas special for fumbling with your best friend's husband in the bathroom, while Morecambe and Wise create a hilarious diversion in the lounge. As the boys sing 'Bring Me Sunshine' the dress rips and the damage is done.

I move on. There is a sixties pea green polyester mini swinging unapologetically beside a Blitz-worn floral day dress with darned underarms, which in turn is beside a strappy-sided fake Versace body-hugger. A quilted, drab dressing gown completes the collection.

Personally, I prefer it when the organisers of these events put these women, and their fabric skins, in some kind of order so that they can hang out with women of their own era at least, women they can connect with. I visualise the rail coming to life, the dresses growing arms and legs, hearts and minds. Having swapped compliments and shared quizzical looks, they would to try to explain themselves. The girl in the thigh-swiping waistless green who is striking the 'broken limb' pose would seem like a cosmic creature to the poor war-torn housewife who had yet to experience victory in the ultimate age of austerity. 'Make do and mend' meets 'Unisex Space Age gear'. Quite a jump.

Fashion evolution is something that has always fascinated me. I hit my teenage years the same year as Sid Vicious joined the Sex Pistols. 'God Save the Queen' roared through our household, drowning out *Songs of Praise* and signalling the end of the age of innocence. It was a short-lived hit in our house. As Sid repeatedly told me that I had no future, my mum flew into the back room and pulled the arm of the record player away. Seconds later, my brother launched a violent counter-attack on the kitchen radio, smashing it against the side of the fridge. Chris says the record was actually The Damned – he still has it, and swears the vinyl has the scratch to prove it. Whichever is true, anarchy had arrived in the Packham household.

In 1977, it was a matter of life and death to belong to a youth culture. Nobody in their right mind wanted to be the same as everybody else, and indeed it was social suicide not to 'be something'. After an uncomfortable strut down the high street in a hobble skirt and itchy mohair jumper, with a Boomtown Rats badge pinned to my chest, I knew I didn't have what it took. I didn't want to look ugly, and didn't know what anti-establishment meant. So I changed in the Woolworths loo and returned home with a bag of pick-n-mix instead.

Before long I became a mod. My first earnest musical purchase was 'Start!' by The Jam, and I had a Jean Seberg-inspired pixie cut. My dad said he wanted to throw a brick through the hairdresser's window when I came back with my new look, but I didn't care. With fashion came courage.

The original mod culture had blossomed in the post-war affluence of the early 1960s. Youths had spending power and a desire for style. This second wave of mods, inspired by the 1979 movie *Quadrophenia,* danced to the new sound of ska mixed with the exciting energy of punk. The look was clean-cut and cool, and the androgynous angle appealed to my mildly rebellious new self. We wore two-tone skirts and Fred Perry T-shirts, with winklepickers and granny coats of camel-hair wool and, of course, white tights. We had boyfriends with mopeds who wore parkas and union jack patches, and we hung out around the bus station. As with all youth cultures, clothing was paramount and, for a mod, finding original items from the 1960s was the holy grail. Before long, I had discovered every charity and second-hand shop in the south of England.

Rummaging through old clothing to find something stunning that fits or inspires is a skill I have developed over many years. Usually these shops ignore the conventional rules of merchandising, and the physical effort required to prise the crushed velvet from the broderie anglaise is so immense that I have developed a sixth sense: I can immediately tell, based on the texture and touch of a shoulder alone, whether it's worth wrenching the hangers apart. The lack of seasonal similarities also contrives to confuse the shopper, with a hectic mix of hotchpotch prints and clashing colours. Meanwhile, the 'highlights' are draped around the walls and dangle from overhead beams, floating at the edge of your vision as you try to make sense of this retail explosion of stuff. It's a booby-trapped cave of delights.

What is needed is a moment of mindfulness. First, one must analyse the floor plan, decode the den's modus operandi and start scavenging. In her brilliant book *The Creative Habit* the American dancer and choreographer, Twyla Tharp, describes this as 'scratching'. But when I plunge my hand, lucky-dip-style, into a mountain of manky silk scarves, 'scavenging' seems to most aptly encapsulate the feral nature of the search.

In more recent years, I have preferred not to mess with the crumpled cast-offs of a teenage closet or the casual separates of a fifties homemaker. I'm looking for treasure, digging for gold, and it's usually 'behind the till' or 'out the back'. I'll introduce myself casually as a designer and the gates to heaven open. A serious retailer would not want their jewels peddled to amateurs.

In New York in 2003 I had a good day. It was bitterly cold as I meandered through downtown SoHo on the vintage trail between Mott Street and West Broadway. My first takeaway was an Ossie Clark jacket in white crêpe with a cigarette burn on the cuff (which lowered the price) and my mind started buzzing with images of Bianca Jagger at Studio 54, carelessly brushing up against Andy Warhol's butt. Later, I succumbed to a black satin crêpe dress, ankle length and with a colourfully embroidered border. It was unusual in both its abstraction and technique, with large loose threads caught between the gold foiled outlines of a wondrous fantasy garden. I held it tightly, paid and left with the uneasy feeling that the vendor had made a mistake and that I would be chased down the street, my beautiful trophy snatched away from me.

Feeling high from my purchase, I made my last stop on Thompson Street. The store was bright and pretty and the satin slip dresses, lace-trimmed camiknickers and silk kimonos on display were fresh and uplifting. I was drawn to a wooden dresser against the wall. Inside, a small early-Victorian capelet grabbed my attention, made of tulle and featuring painstakingly woven orange blossom around the scalloped hem. Such intricacy is seldom found, and its fragility was appealing. However, it would be of little use to me as I could never replicate such work, and I would have moved on had I not noticed a small handwritten note attached to the collar. 'Worn on my wedding night – handle with care!'

It was mine.

The shop assistant wrapped the cape carefully in tissue and we chatted about its uniqueness. I promised to take good care of it and returned to my hotel. But when I got back to the UK it was gone. Somehow its lightness between the sheets of tissue had tricked me, and I had carelessly left it in a paper bag that I had tossed into the corner of my hotel room. I imagined it dumped in the trash can at the back of the hotel, doused with the restaurant's scrapings, damp, stained and lost forever.

The gown I bought that day turned out to be one of those once-in-a-lifetime finds. A few years later, I found an image of the same dress in a vintage collector's book. It was one of ten images depicting the 1920s, a couture piece by Georges Doeuillet, a French designer who was given the Legion of Honour for his contribution to fashion. A decade ago, it was worth $3,000. However, I can never separate my luck from my loss that day. In the capelet I had been entrusted with a legacy and I had let the side down. A bride's wedding trousseau folded and loved for a century, passed from one woman to another, had kept a memory alive, and I had lost it.

When I trawl the vintage stores, I am looking for beauty to recycle and make my own. I'm searching for a new colour, an extinct shape, the Golden Fleece of fashion. I have a postcard on my bedroom shelf that embodies this idea for me. It is an image from conceptual artist Sophie Calle's installation at the Metropolitan Museum, a black and white photograph of a young man with a heavy fringe covering his eyes. The artist exhibited a series of photographs of blind people and asked them to describe their image of beauty. Beauty is an overwhelming concept for everyone. Is beauty timeless or something that burns brightly for a moment; is it symmetrical perfection or decaying splendour? Whatever form it takes, the agreed definition is that it pleases the aesthetic senses – especially the sight – and this is the essence of my work. The postcard nudges me to continue the search, to retrieve and create my idea of beauty with the hope that, one day in the future, what remains of my passion, my designs, will be discovered in the back room of a vintage store in Los Angeles waiting to ignite and give life to yet another dress.

Vintage shopping not only provides me with an endless resource of ready-made details, potential print references, embellishment ideas and exciting colour combinations. It also enriches my work through my fascination with the lives of the women who owned and wore my collected treasure, bringing them to life again. That too inspires me.

A few weeks after my interview with the journalist I do have an idea for the next collection, and find that my inspiration comes from a woman I know virtually nothing about, despite her legendary status. But it isn't the first time I've encountered her. Five years ago in the Museum of Hollywood, just off Sunset Boulevard, I had discovered a cabinet dedicated to Jean Harlow. At the time, I was on a search for Marilyn memorabilia as she was the muse for my spring/summer 2015 collection, so I only stopped long enough to gather that Jean's life was yet another Tinseltown rags-to-riches tragedy. In true Hollywood style, the script is sprinkled with controversy and intrigue: Jean was dead by 26. After two months of marriage her director husband, Paul Bern, shot himself, leaving a cryptic note, and his ex-wife Dorothy jumped to her own death two days later, igniting murderous gossip that never quite left Jean. A few years later she collapsed on set, suffering from the late stages of undetected kidney disease, and slipped into a coma. Jean's cramped display case of fading snapshots and small typewritten notes, all portraying a life less ordinary, stayed lodged in my mind.

Perhaps it was a blonde moment; I was drawn to Harlow's chromium curls while scanning the exhibits for Marilyn's peroxide quiff. She was Hollywood's ground-breaking blonde, who became known as a bombshell after the success of a screwball flick of the same name in 1933.

The following evening, quite by chance, I checked into the Jean Harlow suite at Chateau Marmont, where the actress slept on her wedding night. It is said that Jean hastily broke her vows and left her new husband asleep to indulge in a tryst with Clark Gable, although that could be just Chateau folklore. The Chateau is in West Hollywood, nestled into the hills beside the Sunset Strip. The iconic hotel, which opened in 1930, is notorious for its scandal-ridden rooms and has always been a hedonistic home for the Hollywood elite. The rooms have been kept in their original style and, in bed that night, it was easy for me to envisage Jean slipping silently out of the other side, wrapping her milky slipper-satin robe around herself and tiptoeing down the hallway to yet another iconic moment.

Meanwhile, during my research for my last autumn collection, I had collected some art deco images. Representing decadence and glamour, deco originated in Paris in the mid-1920s from a recipe of cubism, Fauvism and enthusiasm and was one of the first truly international styles, influencing design from factories to fashion. The strong

21

interlocking lines combined with elegant curves work beautifully across the body, creating flattering symmetry, and have been reproduced by designers ever since. There is a timely connection between Jean and art deco that makes everything fall into place in my mind. Jean's glamorous portraiture, swathed in silver screen satins, and the decadent drama of the thirties skyscrapers, fuse perfectly and I decide to continue my research into her life.

Among the multitude of Harlow biographies I found Jean's own novel, *Today is Tonight,* online. Yet more controversy unravelled. The book was not published until 30 years after her death and there are questions over its authenticity. I waved that notion aside – I wanted Jean to have written it – and clicked 'buy' immediately. It is melodramatic and lovable trash. The plot is ridiculous yet irresistible: Judy and Peter lead a life of luxury in the Roaring Twenties. Then they lose it all in the Wall Street crash and move to a house with no room to swing a cat. Peter becomes blind after an accident and, not long after, Judy gets offered a job posing nude as Lady Godiva at a nightclub. Her husband would never approve, so she sets up an elaborate plan to turn day into night and night into day so that he doesn't realise she is working the graveyard shift to earn the desperately needed money.

I like the idea of calling the show 'Today is Tonight'. It means something and nothing. It has its own story but it is also vague enough to be ours. It suggests glamour, but leaves plenty of room for my own interpretation.

So I have Harlow, whom I am beginning to adore, and I have art deco. Hollywood glamour and architecture are very obvious inspirations and I have indulged in them before. But Jean brings something a little different .

Jean and her wardrobe are synonymous with the evolution of power dressing and for me encapsulate the sense of liberation felt by women at that time. Art deco meanwhile zigzags from Sonia Delaunay's crafty concentric circles to the gleaming phallic, piercing summit of New York's Chrysler Building, obliging me with endless possibilities for surface embellishment.

However, the relevance and originality could be questioned. Explaining my sudden interest in Jean is difficult to justify. I could just as easily have collected pigments from J.W. Waterhouse's Pre-Raphaelite muses sweetly doing nothing, lounging on velvet cushions and plucking the petals from wildflowers, or taken a moped ride around 1960s St Tropez watching the boys watch the girls in their white bikinis. Sometimes the onset of inspiration can't really be explained.

I must trust my intuition, and allow Jean to pull me into her world. I take this literally for a moment and imagine myself at the Metropolitan Studio in 1930, on the set of *Hell's Angels*. An American aviation epic, it was one of the most expensive films made to date and Jean's cinematic debut. Jean, 18 and lithe, is striding ahead of me, waving at the crew and heading towards the producer, the movie mogul Howard Hughes, and James Hall, her leading man (also rumoured to be her latest love). I imagine myself as her funny friend from the future as she steals me away to her dressing room for a Gin Rickey and a tour of her costumes.

Conjuring up images of the interiors is easy. I can almost smell the white calla lilies in their French deco crystal vase obscuring the large circular mirror of a maple-wood dressing table. On the floor is a heavenly row of pretty T-bar pumps; black suede with tiny multi-metallic straps, silver lamé-toed slippers with diamanté edging and a dusty rose-coloured taffeta pair finished with a tiny crystallised ball dangling from the ankle strap. I would love to squeeze my twenty-first-century-sized feet into them but know better than to try.

As I turn up the hem of a lamé dress I find draped over a chair and study its finishing, Jean begins an animated monologue of girly gossip. She turns to face the mirror and pulls off the lid of her Max Factor Harlow ruby lipstick, and I take the fantasy further, stepping into Jean's skin and swiping the cream rouge onto *our* lips in a coquettish bee-stung style. Our face is powdered white, lashes long and heavy with Maybelline mascara. Those legendary high-maintenance eyebrows are tweezed thin and arched high and, as I try to push my hand through my hair, I am surprised by the rigid waves, sticky and shiny, fixed with sugar and vinegar. I stare at our reflection.

'Would you be shocked if I put on something more comfortable?' I mimic her most famous one-liner, yet to be immortalised, and wearing nothing but a canary yellow silk dressing gown I pull tight the sash around my little waist and give myself a wry smile.

But that's enough of the method designing.

Like the Fox executives who signed up Harlow without a screen test, I am sticking close to this goddess. However, the moment of inspiration needs that extra energy that will fuel the imagination of the audience and bring the theme up to date and beyond. I want the attention-grabbing ideas that will get the collection noticed. It's a show, a creative performance, our livelihood. It would be so easy to create a beautiful collection of thirties-style evening gowns but, while there should be a strong influence from this era, it will not be enough.

I discover more starlets, Clara Bow and Barbara La Marr. They seem entangled with each other. The *Bombshell* film plot was allegedly a tale of Bow's manic life and Harlow's husband Paul Bern was rumoured to be the father of La Marr's son. Like Jean, these girls were living fast and furiously. They were the It girls of their era, eating up life, bingeing on fame. In front of the camera they were defining a new form of femininity, setting the bar for beauty, flaunting their sexuality and trampling on social acceptability. The depression-era world lapped it up with their popcorn and soda.

In *Hell's Angels*, Jean's charming but immature acting style is eclipsed by the silk evening slip that barely covers her breasts. The 'pre-code' gown by legendary studio designer Howard Greer undoubtedly enhanced the strength of young Jean's box office appeal.

Pre-code Hollywood, I discover, was a brief uncensored pocket of cinematic history between 1929 and 1934, when the 'talkies' started and the immorality guidelines were limp. The movies made in this period were liberally spiced with sexual innuendo and provocative dressing and feel strangely avant-garde in our #MeToo world.

It's easy to romanticise their wild lives, but behind the scenes these vulnerable young women were trying to grow up in a town that was sucking up their youth in exchange for celluloid immortality. In black and white, their lives were idyllic with amusing dramas and happy endings. But in real life, they were riding a full technicolour rollercoaster, disillusioned in love and on a studio diet of frivolity and fear.

I am interested in a modern take on the It girl theme. The term seems to have originated in the early 1900s, when the novelist Elinor Glyn used it to describe the intangible attractiveness of some men and women. A true It girl is undoubtedly beautiful and stylish, but as I trawl the list of crowned Its, there is a vulnerability in their eyes that connects me to them. I am sure that even if I didn't know the tragedies awaiting legends Harlow and Monroe, I could sense the sadness in their beguiling images. And of course, from Britney Spears to Lindsay Lohan, we find inspiration in the fragility of It girls to this day.

To contrast the perfectionism of Hollywood with the sumptuousness of art deco *and* the fragility of early fame helps deepen the plot, and begins to give me styling ideas of messy hair and smudgy eyes, that 'just got out of bed' look, with models sauntering a little undone down the catwalk to softly played piano tunes, as if floating from the set of a silent movie. A little provocative sabotage is needed, a hint of deliberate deconstruction. A bit of Hollywood reality. This reminds me of a quote from F. Scott

Fitzgerald's *The Beautiful and Damned*: 'The fire burning in her dark and injured heart seems to glow around her like a flame.'

As I write this, I am imagining eau de Nil crêpe and smouldering snow-coloured satins, and plunge-back black draped bias dresses with tulle inserts. Dressing for early monotone cinema took particular skill. With artful detail, bold patterning and clever use of tone, the dresses from this era are some of the most iconic in screen history. The leading lady mesmerises the audience with a shapely silhouette light in colour and rich in detail as the supporting cast form a backdrop of dull grey and black illuminating the star.

Search Harlow's publicity images and it's evident that she spent almost the entirety of her screen career dressed in ghostly white satins and silver-sequinned chiffon in angelic shades.

Ultimately, I decide to opt out of this palette and add vividness, mixing ice cream pastels and splashing the collection with ruby red and cobalt blue, interspersed with a final nostalgic dash of black and ivory. After all, inspiration shouldn't be too obvious in the final product.

For example, Van Gogh collected prints by Japanese artists, notably those by Hokusai and Hiroshige. At the Van Gogh museum in Amsterdam, I followed his love of

Japanese art from undiluted imitation to a mere change in perspective indicative of one of his Japanese predecessors. Now, in every Van Gogh, I search for the Japanese aesthetic. 'After some time, your vision changes, you see with a more Japanese eye, you feel colour differently,' Vincent's brother Theo wrote to him in 1888. Van Gogh used the inspiration within his *own* style, adding depth and balance amid his wild brushstrokes. Nothing is truly original, so the aim is to create the appearance of originality through the amalgamation of good ideas generously donated by history with innovative creativity.

So, that's how it begins. Ideas are blurry, and inspiration is open to interpretation. Spoiled with beautiful and rich resources, we can begin to design, extracting the colour from a slipper, the cut of a sleeve or the teen spirit of our muse.

I revisited the Museum of Hollywood as I was finalising the collection. They have a new Jean Harlow exhibit now. The centrepiece is a large painting of Jean that her mother commissioned after her death. I am not sure how I feel about Jean's mother, also named Jean. Her controlling influence litters the pages of Jean's history, possibly hastening her daughter's demise. Even as Jean lay dying, legend has it that her mother struggled with the idea of medical intervention due to her own religious beliefs. The painting, by P. Tino Costa, was lost for 50 years and discovered by two sisters in a raccoon-infested, dilapidated house. In it, Jean is wearing a sheer white gown and has her hands characteristically thrown above her head, her way of saying goodbye. The title of the painting is *Farewell to Earth*, and around Jean's waist is a pale pink band. Below the painting is a placard explaining the symbolism of the image: Jean disliked pink intensely. Jean's mother knew that and, thinking of the tension that must have passed between them, I feel suddenly tired of the relentless drama that seems to define every detail of Harlow's life and beyond.

Strangely, as the season progressed, our plans for the collection to be shown in the ballroom at the Mandarin Oriental Hotel in Knightsbridge fell through. A newsworthy fire broke out on the top floors and the hotel was closed for months, forcing us to relocate to our Mount Street store for a more intimate presentation. I was disappointed, but it crossed my mind that this mild disaster was almost in keeping with the collection's inspiration reflecting the troublesome life of my muse.

I have all I need from Jean now. Her brightness prevails, overcoming the darker side of her glamorous stardom, and I am in awe. The power to inspire almost a century later is surely a reflection of an extraordinary life. As I turn my back on the painting and depart, the final dress of the show comes to life in my mind. It is white, ethereal and sheer, with a sparkling rose-coloured ribbon around its waistline, and I imagine for a moment that perhaps it may find its way back to Hollywood to be worn by another shining star – an It girl who likes pink.

FABRIC

The battery-operated hand-held sewing machine (circa 1979) was a foolish purchase. My inability to save was unfortunately compounded by my impatience and I had eventually nagged my parents into a loan. The advertising campaign had caught my imagination and I watched in awe as the nifty machine ran up the sides of curtains and whizzed around the hem of a skirt (while the model was still wearing it). These gimmicks intrigued me, but I had other plans for my new appliance. I envisaged sewing up my latest designs in the back seat of the car as we sped away on family outings and when, at 5pm, the dining table was needed for supper, instead of packing up I would just continue – on the floor or even in mid-air. With this machine I was going to pursue my work in spite of the family time-table. However, stitching a straight line with this newfangled invention was like climbing without ropes – it required a high level of concentration and any small shift in thumb tension could lead to disastrous slippage. As an idea it had potential, but did it really make sense to sew on the go?

Many things in life can appear to make no sense if we analyse their purpose, but we are apt to do them anyway, and never more eagerly than when we are young and brave. Naivety and blind ambition can be a beautiful antidote to the unsought words of experience from those who know better. By raging against common sense and smothering pessimism, dreams may have wings to fly. So, in 1987, when I decided to start a luxury fashion house in a small studio under the Westway, with a boy I had been kissing for less than six weeks, it made no sense to anyone but us.

The Westway is a section of the A40 dual carriageway running between Paddington and North Kensington. The studio was tucked under the flyover and a few moments' walk from Portobello Green – the happening end of the Portobello Road. It was the place to be and every other coffee run would be punctuated by a close encounter with the idolised of the time: Mick Jones, Joseph Fiennes, Rupert Everett and Annie Lennox would be jumping the queue at the local café for their caffeine hits as I fell behind to eavesdrop and stare. And the boy I was kissing? Mathew with one 't'. A handsome sculpture graduate with musical fingers and deep blue eyes, he played me into his heart on the first beat. We had first met four years earlier on the spiralling staircase of Central School of Art during a graduation show opening night and, after a few words, had gone our different ways. Given how our life together would unfold, that fleeting collision on the stairs is remembered with fondness as one of those moments when nothing and everything happens – the plot twist still under wraps.

As I reminisce about how our business began, I stop to think about ambition. It is a common perception that ambition is triggered by a fear of failure or not being good enough and, while I recognise these traits in myself, I don't agree that to have a dream and pursue it with determination and passion is a response to low self-esteem. Recognising your own destiny is surely a lucky break. However, I do think the growth of ambition depends on a complex construct of factors.

My own sense of ambition may have been jump-started by an overachieving brother. Chris is four years older than me, and as a child he would chatter incessantly, seemingly without stopping to breathe. My early memories of him run like Super 8 film footage, where an excess of frames per second causes things to play fast – and he did, whirligigging around my pram, flying plastic dinosaurs across my view and catapulting in the occasional worm. Chris's hyperbolic enthusiasm for life set light to my world but left me speechless, submissively mute until I was three and a half. When I did break my silence, he just upped his game and, while I worshipped the earth he flicked in my face, I developed a stealthy approach to sibling rivalry by devising a cunning plan to eventually sideline any unnecessary competition by finding a talent within myself that didn't interest him. So, at school I scratched at the strings of the violin until I was asked to leave the class, mimed in the local choir and dizzily spun my pirouettes in the back row of ballet classes. But one night as we drove home from the Christmas school show the collective sniggering of my family knocked the stardust from my eyes as they mocked my performance as the disjointed back end of the nativity's donkey. Maybe the self-inflicted humiliation of my have-a-go youth, propelled by my desire to find my passion, served me well. For even now when I find myself challenged, I ask myself: what's the worst thing that can happen?

Given my desire to have a parallel existence to my brother, combined with my mother's dedication to creating a world of possibilities and my father's abiding belief that giving up is not an option, it is not surprising I started my own business. To be nobody but yourself and to embrace the difficulties of life were my takeaway messages from an exhausting childhood.

Therefore, on Sunday afternoons it wasn't unusual to find us searching out a stream in a dappled green glade of the nearby New Forest with the intention of building a dam. Left alone with 'a job to do' we would be consumed with beaver-like dedication, foraging for sticks and stones, first placing the largest in the babbling shallows, and then by plugging the weak spots with mossy pebbles and crumbled leaves we would work to complete the task – to stop the flow of water and hold back time before we dam-busted the stream and returned home. The memories of these captivating afternoons have encouraged me to believe that success can be achieved through dogged persistence and finishing what you start. Whether ambition is nature or nurture is a mystery but, either way, if you handle it with care, it can be expansive.

But how does it feel, that inescapable force of ambition, in my body? I try to draw it and, as my pencil moves around and around on the paper, I form an egg-shaped solid. I press hard with the pencil and the form is smooth, dark and hard. I know where it lives – lodged in my chest like an extra organ, its gentle curves pushing against my heart. A therapist friend remarked that she sees ambition as a diamond and, while I prefer the idea of a brilliant-cut treasure (preferably larger than the Koh-i-Noor) implanted within me, it's too bright and sparkly – for ambition doesn't always shine.

Ambition does not exist without sacrifice and I have often resented its presence, despaired at its persistence and unnegotiable ways and, at times, imagined a life without the constant threat of underachievement or failure. Online forums discuss the benefits of healthy ambition and the pitfalls of blind ambition. But it appears to me that success is often derived from tunnel vision and is a question of how far you will go and what you are prepared to risk. We all have ambition, but it is the level of our aspirations that may predict the potential to win or fail. While some are too scared to even dream, others are willing to surf the extremities of human vulnerability. My own ambition has its limits and exists within the nucleus of my work. At home, it doesn't bother me that I am incapable of making a decent sponge cake and the fact that I can't touch my toes after four years of yoga is nothing but remarkable, but the disarrangement of a burst of beaded flowers trailing across the bodice of a bridal dress or a badly turned hem may cause me to lose sleep.

In the early days of our relationship, Mathew and I huddled in the corners of Notting Hill's cafés, drinking tea and scribbling on serviettes the designs for a small collection that would make us rich and famous – and then we would share our loose change to pay the bill. To have a creative life together was our theory of everything and, looking back, I can only smile at our blissful ignorance of the path we had chosen.

Our first collection was just 12 pieces and I am struggling to describe its 'look'. It was a playful range of evening wear inspired by a trip to Barcelona, a homage to the Spanish abstract artists of the fifties and a hot summer night on Las Ramblas. Strapless tutus with circular satin skirts printed with striking silhouettes of Spanish guitars, tiered hip frills striped with a design of piano keys and boleros dotted with musical notes. A one-hit wonder, some may have thought.

However, within weeks of completing the collection I miraculously managed to get an appointment with Lucienne Phillips, a luxury multi-brand boutique in Knightsbridge and one of the first 'designer' shops in the UK. I was taken aback by its seventies décor: the thick pile carpet had lost its lustre, worn away I suspected by the twirling of Joanna Lumley and other fabulous style icons of the time. But I was surrounded by the best of eighties fashion from designers Bill Blass, Geoffrey Beene and Jean Muir so, as I began to unpack my little 'Flamenco band' collection from the garment bags, the plucky confidence of my 23-year-old self began to deflate. However, Lucienne had a reputation for spotting new talent, and her shop window was the one to watch, so before long I too found myself twirling – modelling the strapless tutu with the revolving guitars accessorised with Doc Marten boots and opaque black tights. I was not prepared for this impromptu modelling job, and I remember glancing at my reflection with its slightly gingery bob and hot-pink lipstick and wishing I had brought a tall and skinny friend with me.

'Your first collection is the only original thing you will ever design,' said Lucienne, diverting me from my thoughts. She meant no malice but her remark turned my eager smile into a perplexed frown – I was going to be original forever, wasn't I?

Lucienne was right, of course; originality is a beautiful rarity often served up by the young and thereafter short-lived. As the creative mind becomes tainted by experience, the inability to distinguish our own ideas from those of others escalates. In the cocooned environment of our studio, commercial naivety had given way to an untethered imagination and, while I cannot claim that even these initial works were truly original, they were fresh and witty. As I unzipped the covers that morning and unfurled my designs for judgement, that noise – the opinions of others – began, and Lucienne was about to start the ball rolling.

*

Lucienne declined to order that day. I suspect she knew that her maturing clientele would pass by my styles with a smile as they made a beeline for their favourite designers, but she must have been charmed by my lily-white enthusiasm, as she offered to put the collection into her window. This was a breakthrough moment for our fledgling brand as the shop window opportunity was the equivalent of, in today's world, a week-long endorsement by a top influencer.

The following season Harrods took the collection and so, with the approval of the world's most famous luxury store, we exhibited at a trade show at Kensington Olympia, hoping to capture more interest. While Mathew manned our stand, I stalked the American buyers – Saks Fifth Avenue, Bergdorf Goodman and Neiman Marcus – and, with my model in tow, zipped around the crowded aisles lining up to casually bump into them. It worked, and on my first trip to New York not long after, I went window-shopping on Fifth Avenue, counting the uptown mannequins in my designs.

When I am asked what have been the highlights of my career I often reply, 'Sandra Bullock in soft pink tulle on the red carpet – our first ever A-lister.' Or I may mention our twenty-fifth anniversary show at the Victoria and Albert Museum, the catwalk running the length of the magnificent Raphael gallery. But, while these were special moments, are they really my highlights? In truth, it would be the memory of Mathew and I speeding to King's Cross at midnight in our Volkswagen Beetle just as the Sunday papers were being delivered, impatient to see if we really had made the front cover with a dress from that first collection and then celebrating with a bagel in Brick Lane. Alternatively, it could be the placing of our first celebrity wear – Wendy James from Transvision Vamp had wandered into our studio one afternoon, taking away a gold and red sequinned minidress to wear for her latest pop video. She sent it back later folded to the size of a postage stamp and rammed into a Jiffy bag. The intoxicating excitement of those first achievements is hard to beat.

Fast forward 30 years and I am sitting in a board meeting at our studio in north London. Mathew is opposite, running through the company's financial position. He looks serious and is explaining to my colleagues his latest predictions, his pencil rolling between his fingers as he gently talks through the impact of the recent rent increases. I flip up the screen of my laptop to check my emails and stop listening for a few minutes.

Earlier in the day we had walked to work across the Heath and as we chatted about the latest profit-and-loss projections a heron had taken flight from the boating pond shoreline. We stopped to watch, enjoying this moment of natural wonder, and as the bird disappeared over the tree-tops we continued our discussion. And this is how it has been for three decades – a continual work-related dialogue interfaced by the rhythm of life.

In the beginning, we were self-employed apprentices multitasking the roles of a very modest company. Gradually discovering each other's skills, we began to divide responsibilities, giving each other autonomy in finance and design. It has not always been easy and often we have fought our way through the multitude of daily decisions with an intensity that might have ended other relationships. We were warned that love and business were tricky partners, but it never felt like a decision from which we could pull away – the seeds sown as our attraction and growing love for each other had taken hold. Even now, I admit to feeling a sense of security in our bonded management of all things and the occasional tension over company matters reassures me that both love and passion are still very much alive.

This may seem melodramatic for a company designing and manufacturing women's evening wear, but perhaps the clue is in the word 'fashion', with its synonyms of craze, mania and fad. The energy required to create a commercially successful product and continually maintain your customers' interest in your brand is relentless, and to be in fashion suggests that there is always a potential to fall out of fashion. It is a rollercoaster ride that needs skilful management.

While other industries may produce a range of products and gradually evolve them, making slight modifications or rebranding, designer fashion companies such as ours are investing in 200–300 new looks per year. Therefore, it isn't surprising that each season, the days leading up to presenting the collection are tense as the reality of our dependency on the success of the designs feels acute: our future hangs in the balance – and on a rail. When a customer arrives in the showroom, they are searching for both novelty and excitement in our work, every season.

So with this in mind we create a 'range plan' for each new collection, and by analysing the trends of the previous season – the attributes of the best-sellers and the notable failures – we carefully put together a board of must-have styles outlining both the design requirements and the financial guidelines for the season. There are few processes in our work that I'll admit to finding difficult, but this is one of them. Others include the front-row seating allocation of a catwalk show and the intense experience of going through the end-of-year accounts. I struggle with big egos and small figures. However, I acknowledge the importance of the plan and so my team and I pool our combined knowledge to form structure around our creative concepts.

Fashion trends can be unpredictable, and trying to second-guess the future desires of an international clientele can feel like stitching in the dark. Initially, the detail of the range plan can feel restrictive – designing with a checklist can tempt you into recreating a popular style, just changing the beadwork or the colour. So, after absorbing all the relevant data, the aim is to design in a way that is both true to the brand and unexpected.

Range-planning a collection is much the same as drafting a business strategy. They are both rolling inventories of past experiences, algorithmic thought and guesswork. A good business plan will become a manifesto, directing daily decisions towards the aspirations of the company in the same way that the range plan sets up the objectives for the collection. They are a means of communicating our direction of travel to both our own team and the outside world. They should be viewed as works in progress, with an inherent understanding that the plan may change – new ideas will pop up to challenge our original thinking and problems will cause us to review our aesthetic ambitions. However, sometimes unexpected events play havoc with the plan and threaten stability.

Fashion is – understandably – one of the first commercial victims of a political upheaval. When Kuwait was invaded by Iraq in 1990 we had just made a shipment to the region and, as the news broke on the radio, we telephoned our customers, not really grasping the seriousness of the situation. The calls went unanswered; they had all already fled. Overnight, evening wear had lost its allure in Kuwait and, as the tanks rolled in, our cash flow was flattened. And when the Russians invaded Crimea in 2014 we were forced to recalibrate our plans for the Baltic region.

Finance as well as politics can affect business; in 2008, on the day we opened our flagship store in Mayfair, the Lehman Brothers bank collapsed, sending the stock markets crashing and so, as we opened the doors for the first time, it was with a sense of trepidation rather than excitement.

While it is true that a small business can respond quickly to such dramas, there is always a vulnerability.

A while ago, Mathew and I split up. The pressures of our little world had caused cracks in our relationship and we were lost. The spark between us had dimmed, smothered by blame and exhaustion. 'We' were no longer top of our priorities and had put our love on hold, thinking it was strong enough to survive, tucking it away under a large pile of must-dos as we got on with running our business. I moved upstairs to the spare room and the strangeness began. As the talking ceased, the sound of a footstep on the stairs, a key turning in the lock, the car engine revving outside in the street became the new mode of communication between us. Our emotional chaos seemed to swirl around the house and we hid from each other. But every morning I got up and went to work and so did Mathew. I cannot be sure if our inability to look at each other, our sharpened tones and clipped conversations or our obliviousness to one another's whereabouts, was noticed, but nobody said anything. I continued making the collection and Mathew did what he always does: he kept the business moving.

The first two months were spent in a kind of shock. A numbness ran through me and my usual sense of care for others fell away as I began to disentangle the events that had led to the inevitable blowout. From my room at the top of the house, I pushed replay and watched what had been, pausing now and again to regret and re-count the days when we had spent more time checking in and flying out than staying home. Meanwhile, voices nattered in my head, our conversations flipping from one year to another, a jumble of joy and jarring chat. For a long time our cross words had gone unsaid; we had zipped them up at work and, as we walked home, we would sidestep each other's snipes. The fear of honesty had made liars out of us, and gradually, as the stress became too bitter, the unsaid words crept into our chat and the accusations began.

Have you ever had that dream where you are naked and strangers are coming to find you? As you fling open the mirrored wardrobe doors, the hangers begin to swing on the empty rails. You desperately pull out drawers, only to find there is nothing there and, with mounting terror, you rip open bags only to find feathers or mouldy rags. And then the door handle starts to rattle. Apparently, this dream of a frantic search to conceal oneself is a sign that you are perhaps pretending to be someone you are really not or that you may be revealing a hidden part of yourself – or even your truest self. I can't be sure whether I was pretending or not, I just wasn't happy. But I did have an overwhelming sensation during the dissolution of our relationship of feeling undressed. As I had exited the room that night having uttered 'it's over', slamming the door behind me, it was as if my clothes seem to fall away from me. I was exposed to the vulnerability of feeling alone.

Occasionally I am asked how I am able to balance the work–life relationship, and I find myself contemplating how I would cope with a more conventional arrangement. I walk the line between all or nothing on most issues that matter to me and therefore our co-joined existence, our resolute sharing of everything, had always suited me. The occasional secret smile between us in a meeting while our colleagues are deep in discussion is my idea of a romantic interlude, a moment of understanding that what really matters still does. To be able to experience the ups and downs of a life designed without partitions was a conscious choice; but what do you do when it appears the whole infrastructure of your life – and the lives of others: family, colleagues and all our adjacent partners – is dependent on a smile? The idealistic dreams of our youth, our combined passions, which had been the foundations of our business, were about to backfire on us.

The convenient arrangement of sharing everything had suddenly become very complex. The idea of having nothing more to do than sell a house, divide the bank account and have a custody battle over the dog almost gave me divorce envy. The reality of prising apart decades of creative togetherness, and potentially blowing apart the business with it, was not a step either of us could take and our sense of responsibility once again took priority. However, the pain of grieving a relationship within such close proximity to each other was inevitably taking its toll. Our business plan was spiralling out of control and I would need to decide what happened next. Mathew wanted our life together to remain intact – to keep both the business and our love alive.

For me, the crushing reality of the seemingly catastrophic fallout that would ensue if I were to give up, and my duty of care to everyone, were my reasons to try again.

So, begrudgingly, and with traces of resentment towards the business, I went back to how it was before – at first more from necessity than choice. In my attempt to separate us, our creative compatibility had been laid bare and now the entwined ambitions that had torn us apart pulled us reluctantly back together.

But things did get better and, as the company celebrated its thirtieth anniversary, we gently rebuilt its foundations – our relationship. It appeared that during the break-up our collected grudges, mismatched thoughts, and our forgetful togetherness had been washed away into the crevasse that had opened and then closed again. Rather than resignation, there was a sense of relief and united sympathy for the pain that had passed. Love hadn't gone, it had just slipped away for a while, bored with us and feeling a little untended.

Of course, love is never mentioned in our business plan, though it is there hovering between the turnover and the bottom line. The delicate balance between creative freedom and financial control and their embodiment in Mathew and myself will inevitably create tensions and swing the outcome of our endeavours. Our passion has fused us and, as we faced the fear of separation, the integral nature of our co-dependency had become apparent and once again we found comfort in its reciprocity.

Whether all long-term relationships should take a break is a matter of opinion. But I think there is a possibility that to take a moment to stand alone between the past and the unknown, to be present and watch the truths of your life unfold, can be valuable. To get undressed for a time and reveal your true self, and the raw nakedness of what it is to be human, can, in a time of pain, give love a chance.

COLOUR

'Grey, what do you think about it?' asked the reporter, pointing up at the sky.

We had discussed the interview questions and this wasn't one of them. This was rather annoying given I was standing in Moscow's Gorky Park live on national television, anticipating a chat about my excitement at being invited to show at Russian Fashion Week. I hadn't yet mastered the art of 'bridging' and so, panic-stricken, I attempted to express my feelings about grey.

'Err ... yes, well, it depends where it is ... ' I stammered, my mind flicking from pebbled beaches to baby elephants.

I could see the young Russian reporter smirking behind his microphone as I spouted banalities as dull as the clouds above me. But, while the grey question was a cunning ruse to put me on the spot and create a moment of awkward repartee, I did leave the scene wondering: what do I really think about grey – or any other colour for that matter?

Our relationship with colour is deeply personal, embedded in our memories and forever evolving. The palette of our lives subtly shifts as the world around us gently recolours itself, and so the complexity of our associations with each colour is as broad as the spectrum itself.

Relaxing in the bath, I study the coral varnish coating my toenails as they peep above the bubbles and I wonder what provoked such a bold choice. I think back to musing over the many tiny bottles in my local beauty salon a week earlier. It had been a rainy evening and, as the fluorescent bulb flickered above me, and the twang of plucked harps drifted from the sound system, I remembered yearning for a little uplift – something 'daring' to brighten myself up. Perhaps it was the lure of the coral's ingredients – a mix of tulip red, lemon and a touch of rose; lust, excitement, happiness and positivity – that took my fancy, or was it my anticipated weekend break to Madrid that had triggered images of flamenco dancers in silky skirts of rosy hues, with peach-coloured blooms tucked up into their hair? Wherever the inspiration had been found, I deleted and selected as I scanned the multitude of pearly, sparkly and opaque shades, paring down my pedicurial desires to reflect my mood without even – consciously – thinking about it.

However, it was not actually such a thoughtless move. As the light-sensitive cells of my eyes' retinas had begun deciphering the wavelengths of electromagnetic radiation bouncing off the multicoloured varnishes, sensory flashbacks had guided me towards my Tango-ed toes.

The way we wear colour is a preoccupation for me. I enjoy women who wear colour well, those who can combine unexpected tones, artful prints and bold accessories. Those who take the time to indulge in self-presentation and to consider how they wish to be received by the world, understanding both the power and pleasure it can transfer. However, it is a skill, and it takes time to find your colours, match up flattering hues and have the willingness to experiment. But those who get it right become walking art, catching our eye and enriching life as they pass us by. The colours we choose to wear say much about our ever-evolving state of mind. So, when we open our wardrobes each morning, we access our options by balancing our aspirations with our itineraries and reach out instinctively for tones to change, reflect or hide our mood. Good sense advises us to prepare the night before, to create our 'look' in order to avoid rushed decisions and sloppy pairing. But I find this rarely works. My focus shifts overnight and I often back down from my pre-planned vibrancy and slip into something more familiar – generally … black.

*

I'm a sucker for fortune tellers. An hour of self-indulgence with someone who can see into my future is a temptation I find hard to resist. I like their cosy rooms with cane chairs hidden by embroidered, fringed throws, and their thumbed-edged cards and crystal balls, simple tools to entice you into trusting in the impossible. I am a cynical believer and yet, like many, I play with the unknown in the hope of a bit of entertainment and a little guidance. Once, I found myself sat in a grubby mud hut on a Gambian beach while an old man who appeared to be speaking in tongues tapped my tummy with a dog's bone and wrongly predicted a pregnancy. And years before, on a park bench in Barcelona, a woman with gold teeth had foretold the value of our next season's order book. I have long excused this strange elopement to the far side as cultural exploration.

So, after a week in St Ives when we and our young kids had exhausted the sights, on a particularly gusty summer's day the mystical bookshop beckoned. Patricia, who was wearing a peachy V-neck chenille sweater, eyed me up, perhaps surprised by my black 'beach holiday' attire. After a mediocre reading promising nothing more than a long life of ups and downs, her most profound utterance was that I wore black because in a past life I had been in mourning for Queen Victoria and 'had quite liked it'. My mother once said, after years of enticing me into clothes that would make me 'stand out', that she realised I wanted to disappear. Neither point of view was accurate. The reason for my departure into the dark years before was that it was cool, flattering and made me feel in control, protected by an impenetrable cloak that could transcend time, class and sex.

The Rothko Chapel in Houston is one of those places I revisit in my mind when I can't fall asleep or when I need a moment to simmer down. While others may mind-travel to lakeside shores and sun-drenched beaches, breathing along with the rolling waves for a moment of meditation, I prefer the solace of Rothko's last earthly project before he took his own life and slipped into the eternal darkness. I have been to the chapel only twice. The first time I was in search of a bit of local culture after a busy trunk show at the local luxury department store. The second time, the chapel seemed to be calling me. In Houston the champagne flows as smoothly as the Texan oil and the ladies who lunch love a bit of sartorial sparkle and glamour as they attend their exhaustive calendar of galas and concerts. So, on this occasion I found myself the special guest at a charity event titled 'Razzle Dazzle goes Royal' (I think I was the royal connection) and, afterwards, suffering from social butterfly exhaustion, I had returned to the chapel to catch up with myself.

The chapel is an octagonal brick building in a suburban area of Houston. Inside there are simple dark wooden benches and 14 large black paintings. They are not completely black; they harbour dark hues that seem to give them an intensity that perhaps black couldn't do alone and, as the daylight filters in around the edges of the skylight, there is light enough to experience the dark brushstrokes made by Rothko's heavy heart. I have visited religious sites in many countries, feeling duty-bound to pay homage to the local saints and the skills of the stained-glass artists and stonemasons who laid the foundations of hope for our God-fearing ancestors. But while I have marvelled at the artistic mastery of the sculpted wings of angels and the Virgin Marys draped in empress blue and framed by twirling gold leaf, I find the décor too over-the-top to tempt me into a spiritual dimension. Rothko's paintings may hang on walls of stark grey concrete, but rather than mere canvases of abstract modern art, they are mesmeric pools of infiniteness, and they appear to pulse.

Within moments of sitting down, my heart rate slows to match their pace; the razzle dazzle begins to dim and I fall fearlessly into my own blissful abyss and as the profundity of human life looms, time seems to stand still. Perhaps I find the honesty of the design appealing. It is comforting in its rawness and lack of ecclesiastical pomp and manufactured hope – the propensity we have to decorate our pain is all but stripped away. Am I making it sound miserable? It's not – it is a temporary sanctuary, a magical Tardis, and a place of peace – in downtown Houston. And it was there that I began to think seriously about the power of the colour black.

It's not an accident that I have flipped here from turning tarots on the Cornish coast to finding nirvana in a Texan suburb. The colour black, the link between my anecdotes, has long been associated with the more serious, unfathomable side of life, notably death and its extensive cluster of related services: undertakers, the occult, the afterlife and even hell. It is mysterious – the stuff of space, black holes and eternity – and perhaps our oldest colour. Originally derived from the soot of burnt bones, it has never lost its macabre allure. The Egyptians, the style-setters of the ancient world, ordained black to be the colour of death. They perfected the creation of black pigment and used it liberally, outlining their eyes with kohl and glossing their lustrous black locks while styling Anubis, the god associated with the afterlife, with a black jackal headdress.

In his brilliant and exhaustive book *The Story of Black*, John Harvey mentions that the raven has had a 'black reputation because it likes lonely places and is glad to eat carrion'. So it appears that our trepidation towards black as the colour of misfortune has also infected our view of black animals and birds. Harvey adds that 'the bad gods could be black gods, and black creatures their creatures; so black cats, goats and ravens became accursèd, and even might be the devil, or a devil, incognito.'

And then I think of bats. My earliest memory of black clothing used with a sense of purpose was when actor Sir Christopher Lee, alias Count Dracula, would sweep his mighty black cloak over the leading lady of a Hammer Horror, shrouding her with his lusty vampirical desires. Lee's portrayal of the Prince of Darkness complicated my early take on cinematic evil by muddling sexuality with jugular draining. Perhaps it was Lee's compelling smirk and big canines that ignited my fascination with black. And I'm not unique: while black does not rank highly on the list of people's favourite colours, it is our number one choice of colours to wear. It suggests superiority and – ironically – individuality, and has come to symbolise power, sexual boldness and mystery.

Black is also a 'coming-of-age' colour. We tend not to clothe our children in black, so when the time comes for them to pull away from us, they choose it to dress up their liberation. So, it isn't surprising that recent youth cultures – mods, rockers, punks and goths – have worn black with a vengeance and by doing so have discovered its empowering properties. Donning black is attention-seeking, but it can also be intimidating, and so provides a perfect shroud for the shy and alternative.

And yet, wearing black is also associated with glamour, elegance and sharp dressing. Many of cinema's most iconic images are women in black: Marlene Dietrich, gender-fluid in her shiny top hat and tails; Anita Ekberg, causing a splash in the Trevi Fountain with her dramatic strapless dress defining her every curve to perfection; and Audrey Hepburn in Givenchy, doused in diamonds and looking cute, forever the LBD poster girl.

I first wore black when I was 15½ years old. Having been invited to a house party in a local block of flats, I stitched up an elegant jersey sheath dress with long sleeves and a slash neck. I had twisted my permed hair into a chignon and backcombed the top, adding 4 inches to my height. Navy blue winklepickers, one long diamanté earring, cat eyes and some damson lippy – I'd never felt so good. That night I met a handsome rockabilly, a gravestone mason from London, and arranged to meet him two weeks later in a basement bar near the bus station. I wanted to look my best, so I made an appointment to have my hair re-permed. As the hairstylist loosened the clips and released the curlers, twisted hair fragments tumbled to the floor, chemically frazzled – but only on one side of my head. So she shaved it away and I left the salon lopsided, frizzy and in shock. A few days later, to divert attention away from my hacked hair, I decided to dye it henna red and to style it with a shapeless 'lumberjacket' in red-and-yellow check, complete with long woolly tassels. Needless to say, the date night at the bar was a disaster. My look had slipped from iconic to demonic and, as I sat downcast on the bus home, I swore that I would for evermore wear black.

At St Martins, I was a black swan, gliding around its corridors of arty paint-smeared walls in a tuxedo and dungarees with a little crest of blonde hair. My prettiness and friendly smile annoyed me – I wanted to be edgy and angular – so I created cheekbones with blusher and scowled at nothing in particular. While my hair colour changed as rapidly as my mood, I stayed dressed in black – navigating the trials of my new-found independence and attempting to exert a confidence I did not yet possess. Black clothing is a practical choice for students; it absorbs spilt drinks, looks good crumpled and easily slides from day into night. Often my only change of look between screen-printing at college and bopping at the local Wag Club was a smoky eye and a brave face. Meanwhile, my work was a riot of colour, and I quickly discovered I liked the neutrality the black provided as a base from which my psychedelic experiments in paint could flow – from dark comes light.

I have felt safe in black, grounded and stylish, comfortable in the colour that says 'look at me, don't look at me'. It is an easy colour to match, and I have found pleasure in working together textures with different weaves and fibres; satin, crêpe and lace. A wardrobe of black provides a multitude of interchangeable possibilities and, as my style has shifted, I have simply added a new silhouette and utilised the adaptability of my monotone classics. But there have been hiccups over the years, when black was just too black.

As a working mother my wardrobe of dark Prada blazers paired with black trousers or a sateen skirt would certainly cut a dash in my world of fashion, but at the school gates I would feel like a Dementor. So when my 12-year-old whispered, 'Please don't wear black to Sports Day,' I relented and bought myself a new lavender silk skirt printed with a trailing silhouette of roses in black. I thought I had cracked it, a perfect compromise that would appease my daughter and leave my style intact.

It was a beautiful afternoon when I arrived at the sports ground and, as I walked across the freshly cut grass, I caught a glimpse of my daughter sprinting towards the finish line. As I got closer, she saw me and staggered to a halt, then turned on her heel and ran in the opposite direction – away from me. I was an embarrassing failure. She wanted me to be 'just' a mum, she later said. Perhaps black represented the part of my life that would take me away from her, the colour that would stop me making play dates and having after-school coffees in cosy cafés. It was the colour of busyness and of my waving goodbye – or was that just my absent mother guilt creeping in? However, I think my negligence was more likely to be in my colour choice. It was the antithesis of a 'motherly' wardrobe, and more than that – in her young eyes black was the colour of witches and villains. Unfortunately, it is not until later in life that the idiosyncrasies of our parents strike warmth in our hearts. I, too, remember freezing in horror as I spotted my own mother behind the school gates. It was only because of her frenetic waving that I had found her at all – and then I wished I hadn't. Why was she wearing a pitch-black Joan of Arc-fashioned wig? Later my brother tossed the thing into the branches of our apple tree – and it was never seen again.

And then a few years ago, post-show and jet-lagged in a hotel room in New York, I found myself idly flicking through my show reviews. On the *Daily Mail* site, the reporter had liked the collection and the images of the catwalk looked vibrant and attractive. However, the last photograph was of me making one of my brief appearances at the end of the show. I grimaced, and scrolled down to the 'comments' section.

'... and the designer looks like a badly dressed nun,' typed David from Milton Keynes. He hadn't thought much of the collection either, but it was his description of me that really packed the punch. Quickly, I went back up to the photograph. My Celine mules and Margiela skirt and jacket were not the usual labels found in a convent closet, yet perhaps David was partially right – my black habit was indeed out of order and I did look like a nun; but surely not a badly dressed one! I vowed at that moment to shake up my wardrobe and purge myself of some of my black. Since then I have let the light stuff in and restyled my beloved black to complement the newness. Occasionally I can be seen in green, blue and even pale pink, and in the summer a pair of printed trousers or a dotty shirt may have their day.

So, intermittently, I remove some unwanted black things from my wardrobe – jumpers, shirts and shoes – and pile them up by the door ready to take to the charity shop. My daughter, now in her twenties, comes to my bedroom and rummages through my cast-offs, taking a few pieces to her room to recycle into her wardrobe of gothic/punk grunge.

She reinvents and styles with youthful inhibition and skill, giving new life to my well-worn garments. But I have to admit, I really do wish she didn't wear so much black – but maybe that's me just being a mum.

*

As I stepped out of the car, the heels of my black patent stilettos sank into the mud. I let out a petulant sigh. Why had I agreed to come and why does everything I do with Chris involve mud? Twenty minutes earlier we had had a near-death experience in the car. A lorry driver had failed to notice us as he appeared to make a last-second decision to swerve onto the slip road, and we had ended up on the hard shoulder facing a hedge. I can remember us laughing hysterically at finding that we were still alive.

It was 1986 and we were about to attend a luncheon to celebrate the birthday of world-renowned naturalist, conservationist and painter of birds Sir Peter Scott. I was the stand-in for a girlfriend Chris didn't yet have and, despite my protestations, I admit to being easily requisitioned when my brother needs me.

Chris had just begun presenting *The Really Wild Show*. He was the new kid on the block and, with his parakeet-style peroxide hair and designer punk garb, about to start shaking up the old guard of tweedy twitchers and get a new generation of kids interested in wildlife. But he knew his stuff and could spot a lesser whitethroat at 100 metres and, having dissected owl pellets on the dining room table for a number of years, he knew a vole's tibia from a dormouse's fibula. Probably why the old boys wanted to get to know him.

I tiptoed across the gravel, following Chris – avoiding potholes and soil-encrusted Land Rovers – towards the Slimbridge Wetland Centre in Gloucestershire. My look for the party was a blend of Siouxsie Sioux and Meryl Streep in *Out of Africa*. I was reinventing colonial style with a pussy-bow blouse and a fitted skirt-suit teamed with my jet-black hair, and a heavy plastering of pale foundation and dark charcoaled eyes. I may even have had a beauty spot pencilled at the side of my lip. It was a bizarre get-up, I admit, but I felt stylish, I felt good, everything was working. Well, nearly – the hat was a problem.

Sir Peter, I later learnt, was an innovative man. Having inaugurated the Wildfowl Trust in 1946, he had dedicated his life to creating a must-go destination for mud-loving waterfowl and by doing so had attracted birds and bird-watching enthusiasts from all over the world. His captive collection flourished too, and soon he was breeding many species of conservation concern. However, one group of water birds, the flamingos, remained stoically celibate. What no one knew at this point was that these birds need to be part of a large flock before they can realise the urge to build a nest and start reproducing. In the wild they occur in vast numbers; millions gather to breed on lakes around the world. Scott pondered this and came up with a cunning plan. He erected mirrors around their pool and tricked them into believing they were in far greater numbers than his modest collection could muster. It worked – they began breeding, Sir Peter's Slimbridge became a hot spot for flamingo fecundity, and to this day they brighten up the place with their fuchsia-coloured onesies.

We were approaching the entrance of the centre when Chris pointed to a sign above the door – 'No Fur Allowed' – and shot me a terrifying glance. 'The hat,' he said, 'get it off – now.' 'What?' I replied, and then suddenly the enormity of my wardrobe malfunction flapped into me. I had a flamingo on my head. Fur or feathers, I was in trouble and as the Miss Marple-styled, clipboard-clutching woman at the door looked up I whipped off my absurd pillar-box hat covered with swirling pink feathers and thrust it into my bag.

That day, I sat next to David Attenborough. I found him to be supremely polite, as I presume he didn't expect to be sitting next to a third-year St Martins fashion student whose interest in wildlife had evaporated forever after being fed a teaspoon of tadpoles by her brother, aged four ... but maybe I was a welcome break from duck, swan or goose talk. Of course, I was totally on edge and, as they all celebrated the extraordinary life and work of Sir Peter, including his ingenious 'Viagra mirrors' for flamingos, I was only too aware of the shocking tufts of plumage glowing in the depths of my bag.

They were just dyed chicken feathers and, on reflection, my masquerading as a flamingo at the table of the world's ornithological elite might have been an apt tribute to Sir Peter's genius, but it could also have cost Chris his career. The fact that it only very nearly happened has always amused us both, especially on a day of life-threatening near misses. It was also a bumper day for new sensory experiences; Attenborough's soft melodious voice and our slow-mo escape from the wheels of a truck were both unique – but it is the vibrant blushing pink of my hat that illuminates my memory and makes me smile. As I picture myself crossing that muddy field in Gloucestershire, I imagine I looked like a very rare bird indeed – a lesser-spotted, pink-crested fashionista!

Marilyn Monroe had more luck than me in flamingo pink. In the 1953 blockbuster *Gentlemen Prefer Blondes*, Marilyn shimmies across the screen in a hot pink strapless sheath dress, matching opera gloves and pendulous chunky diamonds, causing a sensation and singing her way into cinematic history. And in *Niagara*, the film noir that catapulted Marilyn to stardom, costume designer Dorothy Jeakins dressed the young actress in two iconic pink wriggle dresses. It appears that it wasn't just diamonds that were this girl's best friend, but pink!

For my spring/summer 2015 collection, I made Marilyn my muse for the season, and for a woman who had been dead for over 50 years she was surprisingly helpful. When I got stuck on a style, I would just ask, 'Marilyn, how would you wear this?' and she would reply in her signature breathy voice, 'Brighter and tighter, Jenny!'

It all started when I saw her image on a postcard rack outside a Parisian street kiosk. There she was, flirting with me in a beaded leotard, tassels dangling beneath her bust cups and over her thighs, and, for a moment, I imagined I was seeing her for the first time. Her seductive pose and smile held me and then I thought: why *is* she still here? I turned away and walked along Rue du Faubourg Saint-Honoré, but before long my attention was caught by a bust of Marilyn in the window of an art gallery. Her hair was turquoise and she was naked to the waist, her breasts sculpted into a pair of symmetrical Mickey Mouse snouts with a wide grin and perky eyes looking down to the tip of the nipple, Mickey's nose. A bizarre rendition but, despite all the cartoon appendages and atomic turquoise candy-floss hair, the sculpture was undeniably Marilyn. Further down the road I spotted a display of matching ivory suit-cases in the luxury leather goods store Maison Goyard. They were slightly soiled, antique and stacked in decreasing sizes, topped with a round hatbox inscribed M. MONROE UNIVERSAL STUDIOS.

From then on, I made it my mission to search her out every day, and to my surprise it was relatively easy. I found her in bookshops, wrapped around glossy hardbacks, forever the cover girl; and in a frame on the wall of my local Italian restaurant, she watched me eat pizza. I had managed to trigger 'frequency illusion' – a phenomenon created by the brain's love of patterns and sequence – and I began to see Marilyn everywhere. We all experience this now and again, and often confuse the reoccurrence of an object, person, sound or word with destiny. I certainly did, and grabbed Marilyn from her heavenly hideout and hung out with her for the season.

So, I began to research, collecting images of Marilyn. I was interested in her wardrobe and use of colour, but as I thumbed through the Technicolor photographs, the mystery of her timeless relevance began to unravel. Her vivacity, radiance and ebullience (all words that mean the same thing, and yet one alone, for Marilyn, is not enough) radiated from the movie stills and promotional portraits and gradually I, like so many before me, fell in love with her.

Marilyn's wardrobe encapsulates the fifties fashion of cashmere twinsets and wasp-waisted bodices, and yet is surprisingly contemporary. This may be partly due to the constant referencing that her iconic style endures and/or the simplicity of her tailoring, but it is the colours she wears that I find inspirational. While her styling revolves around her sumptuous figure, never deviating from emphasising her curvaceous assets, her use of colour is impactful and fade-resistant – she looks as fresh today as ever. In black, white and the metallics, she honed her sex appeal and left a legacy of scintillating fashion highs, but in colour – pretty mint green, aquamarine, juicy orange, cherry and the perennial pink – she is effervescent, posing in a rainbow of sunshine shades. It is in these images that I find myself connecting to her most, and I start fantasising about how it would have been if I had met her and designed for her and the colours I might have chosen. Curiously, the vibrancy of her wardrobe appears to intensify towards the end of her life, when she developed a passion for fruity-coloured Pucci jersey, and in *The Last Sitting* – Bert Stern's legendary series of photographs, the last to be taken before her untimely death – Marilyn bookends her life in colour by posing naked behind a piece of delicate rosy-pink chiffon. Was she dressing herself up in beautiful hues in an attempt to mask her fragility at a time when she was anything but in the pink?

Recently, a friend gave me a photograph of the Queen. I thought it was an odd gift at the time but I put it up on my studio wall. It is a formal portrait; the Queen is wearing a baby-pink crystal-encrusted gown with a blue sash and a dash of crimson lipstick. And then, a few days later I found an image of Marilyn and I pinned it up beside the Queen. I took some time to look at them; they are both iconic women whose captured moments are scattered across our daily lives, so much so that we are almost oblivious to them. While Marilyn playfully swoons towards me in a cerise halter-neck dress, the Queen looks on, stoically regal – and it's true, they are the antithesis of each other. But there are similarities too: the silvery coiffed hair, the conspicuous relationship to diamonds, a fifties formality in dressing; and, moreover, they are united in their distinctive brand of unabashed glamour. But as I turn my back on them, switch off the lights and go home, what really resonates is the conscious and clever way they wear colour.

A few years ago, I went to a tea party at Buckingham Palace. A large crowd had gathered across the Kelly-green lawn, lining the sides of what I guessed to be Her Majesty's route from the palace to the tented pavilion at the other end of the garden. I had just nipped back for a second serving of cucumber sandwiches when I sensed a dip in the chatter behind me and I turned to see Her Majesty appear on the horizon, standing at the top of the palace steps. However, what I actually saw was a small smudge of powder blue set against the cloudy-coloured backdrop of the palace walls. I ate my sandwiches and gulped down my Earl Grey tea as I calculated whether I had time to get into position for the walk past. My appetite had cost me dear and I soon found myself floundering behind a flock of feathered fascinators and straw trilbies. I don't think it's the done thing to muscle in at such an event but I turned sideways and shuffled towards the front pretending to look for my husband – whom I had actually lost, but finding him by then had become secondary to my determination to see the Queen. I didn't make it to the front, and as the Queen and her entourage passed by, I caught only glimpses through the crowd, slices of dove blue, jigsaw-like fragments of her dress, coat and hat that I would later piece together to make a Queen.

Everyone there that day will say they had seen her – but had they really? I didn't actually see her face and, given the effort I had made, shamefully pushing myself forward, I doubt many others did either. What we did see was what she was wearing, and that had felt sufficient.

The Queen's public wardrobe is a carousel of carefully curated colours worn entirely for the purpose of being seen, of being 'easy to spot' – it is an act of benign dressing. The power of colour to leave an imprint on us is a styling technique learnt by political leaders, celebrities and royalty alike.

For those in the public eye, a wardrobe of colourful, visually interactive ensembles will not only demand our attention but improve their chances of being remembered.

When I start a collection or a bespoke dress, colour always comes first. The occasion, the season, the inspiration must all be considered, but choosing the shade is, I believe, the most instinctive part of the process. The colour of a style will not only leave a lasting impression but can relay both what we wish to say about ourselves and what we would rather not. In those first moments of being seen, it is the artificial aura of the colour we have chosen to wear that will encourage others to make assumptions about us. Therefore, it is quite common when I first meet a client to discuss a design for her to have a definite idea of the colour she wishes to wear rather than a silhouette or fabric. And I am no different. When I am asked to a party, wedding or any other occasion that requires me to 'dress up', colours instantly pop into my head as I contemplate the event and then step back to judge the appropriateness of my initial thoughts. On receiving an invite to a garden party hosted by a bee conservation charity, I remembered a blouse I had seen in a shop window the night before – a yellow one that I could team with a black polka dot skirt. The idea sent me buzzing off into apoidean dressing, researching flowers bees love – hyacinth, calendula and wild lilac – and imagining a clutch bag entirely covered with silk blossoms. And then I stopped, calmed down and restyled my amusing school fete fancy-dress get-up. I tried to take a more sophisticated approach, and in my mind I ran through my wardrobe looking for floral dresses or blouses in blooming shades or honey hues, and made a note to spray myself liberally with a floral scent.

In selecting a palette of colours for a new collection I need to consider skin tones and cultural trends, a myriad of occasions and a multitude of women. For me, to understand the nuances of each colour helps me to design, and to create styles that can both empower and inspire. I design for women who want to become an unforgettable version of themselves and therefore the shade I choose will be intrinsic to the success of the style.

The collection must look fresh, so the design team collect colours and we shuffle tints, hints and shades, imagining them in satins, sequins and chiffon. And although our dresses are generally chosen as individual pieces for special occasions, the collection must blend together like a beautiful bouquet, gently flowing from one shade to another, reflecting the inspirational mood, and attracting the customer – like bees to honey.

But wearing colours can also have a profound effect on our mood. In her beautiful book *The Secret Lives of Colour*

Kassia St Clair recounts a series of experiments made in the US in the late 1970s that involved trialling the calming effects of bright pink on prisoners and delinquents. When painted on the walls of their prison cells and correctional institutions, the colour appeared literally to 'sap the strength of even the toughest man' and there was an immediate drop in violence between the inmates. Does this explain why pink has been worn by some of the most seductive women in history? And was Marilyn's reputation for making men go 'weak at the knees' more than hypothetical?

Perhaps colour can even shape our lives. In 2006, we created a dress for the Italian actress Caterina Murino for her character of Solange Dimitrios in the Bond film *Casino Royale*. It was our second Bond dress; the first was worn by Rosamund Pike in *Die Another Day*. That dress was on screen for mere moments before it became unfastened and slipped to the ground in a crystal puddle during the sex scene with Pierce Brosnan. Determined not to lose another dress to Bond's seductive dexterity, we laced this one up with satin ribbons, which criss-crossed the low-cut back and pulled the bias-cut front taut. Caterina's character miraculously manages to stay in the dress but, tragically, she is tortured and left for dead, tangled up in a hammock on the beach – the dress intact. However, in real life the gown has happier connotations for the actress.

'That dress,' Caterina told me, 'changed my life forever, I became famous and every woman on the planet envied me.'

The film's costume designer, Lindy Hemming, had requested the style in a sizzling shade of pomegranate red, and the combination of the colour, cut and Caterina's curves set off a flurry of calls from would-be Bonds around the world requesting the same style for the women in their lives. Even now we still get the odd call asking after 'the red dress'. Red is the colour of passion, seduction, envy, danger and blood – a perfect Bond film colour on all counts – but for Caterina, it was the colour of success.

'If you need to cheer yourself up, buy a lipstick,' my mother would say when I was young. At the time I took this suggestion as proof of her lack of understanding of my broken teenage heart or menstrual malevolence. But I have found it to be a helpful trick. To take the time to think of your appearance, to try different shades, and then to treat yourself in a relatively cost-effective way can literally put the smile back on your face. The desire for the perfectly coloured pout – a frivolous purchase to lift our spirits – is a well-known feminine antidote to difficult times. In the Great Depression and the world wars, lipsticks brightened, and a carefully applied bold red became a symbol of defiance. Colour's ability to lift our mood is easily forgotten as we hastily reach into our wardrobes in the mornings. But, maybe there is more to gain than just a passing compliment. Experimenting with colour, even just a lipstick shade, can transform our outlook and interaction with the world – and can sometimes even change our lives.

SKETCH

I once jokingly devised a seemingly impossible plan – to get myself and a co-conspirator invited to a party hosted by the hip-hop mogul P. Diddy. I dreamt up this fantasy on a midwinter's afternoon as I sat sketching gowns in my studio in north London. Gazing out of my window at the cloudy skies, I envisaged us gyrating in the thick of a throbbingly cool get-together on Diddy's luxury yacht as it skimmed the Miami coastline, the sun slowly slipping into the ocean. I giggled at the absurdity of myself rubbing up against bikini-clad models and muscle-bound rappers as the boat bounced to the bassy beat of Lil Wayne. It was an unlikely invite but the idea somehow stuck and I would playfully question whether I could make it a reality by focusing on the idea and taking decisions that would lead me in the right direction; and eventually I did.

Some time later, I stayed with my team at the Thompson Hotel in Los Angeles – a short distance from Rodeo Drive, the immaculate nucleus of LA. It's the kind of place where earplugs would be left on the bedside table by way of a polite apology in advance of the hotel's notorious nightlife. A hotel where I found myself looking into the mirror and wishing I had the LA glow and the thrown-together glamour of the female guests who trickled into breakfast sucking up freshly made smoothies en route to their early-morning yoga. One night I chatted to a woman in the lift wearing a tiny gold bikini and sipping a brightly coloured cocktail. Not knowing quite what to say but attempting to ease our awkwardness – or rather just mine – I asked her what she was drinking.

'A Slow Comfortable Screw Against the Wall,' she murmured, taking another sip.

'Is it nice?' I replied, wishing the doors would open soon.

The following day, after research shopping in the vintage stores of LA, we entered the dingily lit hotel foyer and as we walked across the floor I noticed that the reception staff appeared motionless, their gaze fixed on the elevator. At that very moment its doors slid open and a towering posse of men in black pushed past us wolf-pack style. For a few seconds, the reception crowd froze, captivated by the mysterious tribe as it glided towards the exit and disappeared into the bright Californian sunlight. Inquisitive but still jet-lagged, we decided to go back to our rooms – we would find out the identity of the strangers-in-the-foyer later. I had to squeeze myself through a stack of amps, speakers and lighting rig blocking the narrow corridor and guessed I was stumbling into the aftermath of a film or music video shoot. When I reached my door a burly man in double denim came out of the room opposite.

'Hello,' I said brightly. 'Did you have a good day?'

'Yeah, pretty good,' he replied in a heavy southern drawl, casually leaning into the doorframe. 'Just finishin' up – been filmin' P. Did's new promo.'

As it dawned on me that I had just unwittingly brushed past 'the man' himself in the foyer, I felt that my fantasy on that cloudy afternoon in north London was tantalisingly close to becoming a reality. It was Hollywood after all.

And then he said: 'Do you wanna come to the wrap party?'

'Err ... ' I stammered, playing for time. 'No thanks.'

And then I went into my room, closed the door and fell onto the bed laughing hysterically. I hadn't even asked if the party was on a yacht. It didn't really matter – I would never have gone, I just wanted to be asked.

The Diddy challenge was an exercise in counting degrees of separation between an idea and making it a reality. I like this game, and while partying with P. Diddy and his crew seemed like a crazy idea at first, it eventually became a tangible possibility. The skill appears to be in planning the route, but what is most important is the initial thought and the passion behind it – after which the journey becomes a series of decisions working tentatively towards the aspiration. In the same way, when I sketch a dress it is merely an idea, a two-dimensional manifestation of a thought. It is a starting point from which I can add colour and bring richness with texture and detail.

The invite to P. Diddy's wrap party was a by-product of an ambition to become temporarily immersed in LA culture. Obviously, it wasn't P. Diddy I wanted to dress, and so later that year I returned to the same hotel hoping to set in motion another more extravagant plan. To meet Dita Von Teese and convince her to let me design for her.

Vanity Fair once called Dita a 'Burlesque Superheroine', which only begins to describe the magical charms of this tight-lacing fetish goddess who can captivate an audience simply by peeling off an opera glove. A seductress of artists and designers alike, Dita is the dream muse – a living work of art. She is the woman who whipped good old-fashioned glamour into the modern age with a juicy union of sparkling burlesque and a kinky touch of polished latex.

A raven-haired beauty with a snowy white complexion and glossed scarlet lips, Dita's makeovers are stolen from the Golden Age of forties glamour; she could indeed be Marilyn Monroe's more edgy kissing cousin. But, while her styling tips are a throwback to Hollywood's legends – Garbo, Lamarr, Charisse and Gypsy Rose Lee – she is her own woman: a pin-up vixen with omnisexual appeal.

Dita's sell-out tours feature highly choreographed cabaret performances, including her signature 'Martini Glass' act – where she strips out of crystal-encrusted corsetry and into a whopping big glass, splashing about in nothing more than a sparkly thong and some nipple pasties. It is pure spectacle, performed to perfection – a spellbinding cocktail of theatrical parody and fashion that leaves the audience both shaken and stirred.

Why did I want to dress her? Well, Dita excites me too. While she is the undoubted priestess of the niche world of burlesque, with her extravagantly designed props inlaid with pure Swarovski, she can also rock the red carpet with her flawless contemporary style. And she's a feminist.

Do you need a moment to think about that? Well, in a recent interview Dita succinctly explains this delectable irony herself:

Telling my story of finding confidence in glamour and looking to the past for a different kind of elegance and sensuality made me an alternative feminist icon.

And it's true. When Dita teasingly removes her costume, layer after layer, stripping and shimmying, rotating her curves and hypnotising us with her sensual sashay, she owns it, pulling the strings of her laced-up corsets – and those of her audience – with flirtatious artistry. This is obvious to the viewer, and therefore the rules of engagement are clear. It isn't surprising that Dita claims never to have had a #MeToo moment in her professional career.

And I thought it would be interesting to work with Dita. Women who have a strong sense of identity are inspirational to work with and the relationship soon becomes a creative collaboration. My work tends to revolve around the idea of what it means to dress in a sensual way, so I thought that by designing for Dita perhaps I could learn a few tricks.

TODAY
IS
TONIGHT

JEAN HARLOW

JEAN HARLOW IS ILL

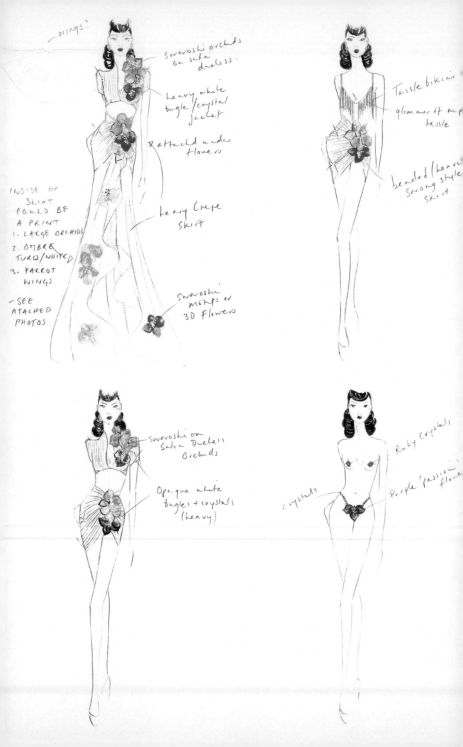

"wings?

Swaroshi orchds
on satn
dress.

heavy white
bugle/crystal
Jacket

R attached under
flower

INSIDE OF
SKIRT
COULD BE
A PRINT
1. LARGE ORCHIDS
2. OMBRE
TURQ/WHITE
3. PARROT
WINGS

- SEE
ATACHED
PHOTOS

Heavy Crepe
SKIRT

Swaroshi
motifs on
3D Flowers

Tassle bikini

glimmer of purp
tassle

beaded (heave
Swrong style
Skirt

Swaroshi on
Satin Duchess
Orchids

Opaque white
bugles + crystals
(heavy)

Ruby crystals

crystals

Purple 'passion'
flower

In 1985 I was bored with wasting time between terms at St Martins and needed to find some work. I already knew that I wanted to design for the nightlife scene so I rang Antony Price, the designer and image-maker celebrated for fashionising rock 'n' roll. He cut Bryan Ferry's brilliantly sharp-edged suits and sculpted Jerry Hall's image by wrapping her in sequinned zebra-skin. He also invented bridge-crutch trousers, which enhanced the phallic bulge, and the rock stars came running, grabbing for a pair. More theatrical than casual, he was an innovative cutter and excelled at eighties glamorous evening wear.

'Hi,' said Price.

'Hello. My name is Jenny, I'm a student at St Martins and I wondered if there is any work I can do for you?'

Three hours later I was having chicken and chips with Antony in front of his television somewhere in Fulham. Those were the days. Sadly, I didn't get to work with him and I have forgotten much of this strange encounter except my unconscious uncoupling from a greasy chicken leg as it slipped onto my lap and something he said that lodged in my mind.

'A woman dresses to either get a man or keep a man,' he told me.

At the time I was irritated by this suggestion. But it does pose the question: what is women's motivation for favouring an off-the-shoulder style with a daring décolletage or for stepping out in a waist-cinching bodycon gown? Why do we exaggerate the female form if not to attract men – and keep them?

While it is clear that Dita dances on the peripheries of seductive dressing, we must all admit to the occasional dabble, employing a few established practices to gain a little traction. We know the tricks and we use them: the careful appliance of lip colour, the thigh-tightening benefits of a heel or the artful flick of mascara to intensify the flutter of our eyelashes. After all, we all have to play the femme fatale once or twice in our lives at least. Bridget Jones's relationship with her support pants versus her desire to wear a smaller pair of knickers is the kind of challenge we all face when treading the fine line between dressing for ourselves and for others.

So, when I'm putting pencil to paper to sketch an evening dress there is a desire to understand what it is that makes a dress alluring. If there is some truth to Antony Price's declaration, it may have had more relevance a century or so ago when a woman's quality of life – and often her survival – was influenced by her ability to capture a man with her wit, charm and ample bosom. Perhaps it was this necessity that triggered the idea that women are competitive – fashion-fighting our way to marital success and security and thereafter protecting our position. Nowadays I believe women dress to inspire each other – and to please ourselves. Women appreciate and admire the efforts of dressing well and we freely give away our beauty secrets, share our shopping tips, as this exchange of information is an integral part of our communication. We are intrigued by our differing styles, and the choices we make in order to express both our individuality and our similarities.

I have yet to meet a woman who says the way they dress is designed to 'keep' a man, although dressing in a way that makes you feel good about yourself will undoubtedly make you more attractive to others. Recently in a vintage shop I was shown a collection of dresses from the 1930s, beautifully packed and never worn. Apparently the relative who had brought in the boxes had explained that the clothes had belonged to her great-aunt and had been bought for her by her husband. The aunt had told her that they were 'simply not her' and had hidden them away intact. It made me wonder – what we would wear if we allowed men to dress us and how would our relationship to other women change?

I am consciously avoiding the term 'sexy', although I do flirt with it during my work day. Within my design studio, we interpret the term in relation to our own brand. Our philosophy of what it means to be sexy is a combination of both my own idea of this and that of our customers, a desire for glamorous charm with a touch of subtle provocativeness. But what does dressing in a sexy way mean? We could start with the practice of foot-binding – an old Chinese custom of binding the feet of a young girl tightly enough to curl them into 'lotus feet'. This painful art of manipulating unformed feet into folded stumps of no longer than four inches was considered a prerequisite to feminine beauty and was surprisingly fashionable for over four centuries before losing its appeal in the early 1900s. While these dainty extremities would limit mobility and often become infected, they were also considered erotic. Covered in small folded slippers of embroidered silk satin, they were considered arousing even as their pained owners tottered around reaching out for support – an early forerunner of the stiletto shoe perhaps, although the modern heel will at least offer you a few hours of uplift before your focus shifts to the pain they are causing. Is it the vulnerability of the lotus feet that triggered sexual attraction in the same way the shape-shifting bodices of the eighteenth century trussed up their wearers, organ-crunching them into submission and leaving them literally breathless? History is brimming with sadistic manifestations of female torture in the name of beauty, but eventually, at the end of the nineteenth century, the hourglass silhouette shattered and women began self-pleasuring; experiencing the softer, uninhibited movement of fabric around their skin, liberating themselves from physically restrictive clothing so they could assert their own sexuality.

My own awakening to the possibilities of dressing your way into the affections of others was sparked by a medley of iconic moments from my youth: Madonna grinding on a gondola like a virgin, lip-biting in black lace; the triumphant Sandy in *Grease* getting the one that she wanted in high mules and tight pants; and Debbie Harry, the peroxide pixie skipping on stage in reckless thigh-splitting tunics. They inspired me to shed my Sunday Girl image and bleach the hell out of my hair.

These women were brave, empowered and winning examples of the transformative powers of dressing to impress. The boys wanted to be with them and we wanted to be them. As a relatively tame teenager, a head girl finalist whose last-minute Sassoon haircut (super-short with a shaped fringe arching over one eye) lost me the title, I took tips from *Top of the Pops* and experimented with new ways to dress – in wearing fishnet tights I discovered I could both rebel against my parents and attract boys, with very little expense and effort. When these transient fashions faltered and I grew up, my most enduring ideals of feminine

sexuality became those of the photographers Helmut Newton and Guy Bourdin. I am drawn to their stylised
composition, their use of minimalist fashion and their
erotically charged scenarios involving strong female stereo-
types. Newton's use of androgynous power dressing and
his naughty-yet-humorous blatancy were a new take on
sexual imagery and style.

What it means to dress in a sexy way is influenced by
our cultural backgrounds, our age, social grouping and
even religious beliefs as well as our personal preferences,
and therefore my contribution to the subject is just foreplay. Cast a glance at the diversity of styles even within
current collections of evening wear and the idea that there
is a formula for designing a beguiling style falls away. Any
designer will soon realise that the challenge is to create in
a more intimate way – to design from the perspective of
the woman, wooing her with the way the garment feels and
moves around her, capturing her imagination and sparking
confidence. We know when we feel good in something:
our posture changes, we stand taller, we stare longer at
ourselves – and forget to look at the price tag. Surely,
whether it be the shapely seamlines contouring her silhouette, an ethereal draping of fine silk, the lightness of a
garment or the form-fitting enhancement of a carefully

constructed corset, the true expression of 'sexy' comes from within. It is, ultimately, whatever turns you on.

Let's get back to Dita.

Prior to my return to Hollywood, Dita had worn a couple of our styles, so asking whether she would be interested to meet me was a long shot but not mission impossible. Our LA agency had told me that Dita was not only her own stylist (preferring to select her own wardrobe) but her own make-up artist and hairstylist too. In a town where your credibility seems to be dependent on the quality of your 'team' – the beautifying experts who smooth away reality to create camera-ready icons – this was impressive.

Before long a meeting was arranged and I found myself back at the hotel, settling down in my pre-booked poolside cabana on the rooftop waiting for Dita. I ordered a drink and tried to relax but, given the imminence of our encounter, I began to panic. What would I say to a woman who has been married to Marilyn Manson and who can go full monty in a crowded room? As I kept busy trying to unearth 'wild nights I wish I'd had' and wondering why I hadn't packed a push-up bra, she arrived, on time, tiptoeing around the pool in skyscraper heels and wing-tipped shades.

A few hours later I told Dita I have to go, I needed to catch my plane home. I never imagined I would have Dita to myself for so long and it felt topsy-turvy me telling her that time was up. Dressed in a hugging blue dress, her hair swept up into a chignon, she was pure Hollywood to me – living proof that the perfection found in the movies of my youth was indeed possible. She has a natural hypnotic coyness and we chatted easily, sharing stories of vintage finds and the secrets of burlesque. Then our mutual love of Swarovski crystals sparked some costume talk and I casually mentioned that I would love to make something for her, my fingers crossed tightly in my lap.

Not long after, Dita did ask me. The costume was to be inspired by Carmen Miranda, the samba-dancing Brazilian Broadway star of the fifties most famously known for her fruity hats and sensational smile. Dita was performing a one-off poolside act for her sponsor and as she revealed the details of her performance my mind started buzzing with ideas. In my studio I began sketching oversized tropical flower heads in pop-art colours encrusted with bright crystals, cascading down the neck-edge of a crop-top worn with a wrapover skirt of white sequins. Most designs usually require some thought about how the piece is put on and fastened, and I found I was enjoying the peculiarities of designing backwards – 'how to strip with elegance' was a new challenge. Dita is a magician – while undoing the hooks she distracts your eye with her saucy wiggle, wriggling free of her fabricated shackles in an effortless twirl, so the careful positioning of magnets and clips is essential to the ease of the tease.

My favourite costume was a design created for her famous 'Lazy' act at the Crazy Horse in Paris. The remodelling of a Jean Harlow wraparound gown in pale blue with ostrich feather sleeves, hand-stitched with thousands of 4mm sequins and light azure crystals, is something most of us would love to slip on when, like Dita, we are feeling just too 'Lazy' to go out. On stage, lounging on a chaise longue in high-heeled mules with matching feather puffs, Dita plays with her manservants and eventually slips out of her gown and into something more comfortable – nothing!

Recently Dita sent me an email with an idea for a new act to be performed at a New Year's Eve show in LA. Dita's visions for her erotic tableaux are always well formed and inspiring, so it isn't long before we are bouncing ideas across the Atlantic.

Hi Jenny!
Sorry I dropped out for a little while been thinking about this
New Year's Eve show idea, and the thing I was thinking of

doing is, well for about 12 years, I had this idea of doing a show where I am a Dita-esque Marie Antoinette coming out of a giant cake, and I actually had started production on it, I have the cake prop that is actually currently all black because I did a fetish cake for Benedikt Taschen's birthday a while back. I also had Christian do shoes but I would revisit it regardless because I kind of have a thing for doing lace up boots with Louis style heels :)

I was thinking of giving the cake a big glamorous makeover, draping it in big sparkly jewels and pearls. This cake is really, really big, I think it stands at about 7 feet tall, and I can sort of climb down the entire thing, it's not like an ordinary bur-lesque cake prop by any means..:)

One thing to note for design is that I come out of the top of the cake, so the dress can't be too voluminous ... I was thinking kind of shortish with small panniers ... do you know what I mean?

Also thinking of colors ... I was thinking of vibrant pastels, like brighter pinks, peridot, canary ... aquamarine ... what do you think?

Hi Dita,
Love the idea of bright colours but I also had a thought that it could be beautiful in white with crystals?

Hope you are good x J
Ps. What do you want to take off? …

Hi Jenny, it will get soooooo dirty … the peachy body makeup
will make a mess of it, I'm afraid!
I'll take off everything but some crystal nipple tassels and a
thong!

For this project I stole inspiration from the 1938 film *Marie Antoinette*. The costumes were designed by Hollywood's star designer Adrian, who, among other unforgettable creations, gave us the most famous shoes in film history – Dorothy's ruby slippers. The fan-flapping female lead was Norma Shearer, whose luminous portrayal of Marie – an eighteenth-century fashion icon – made this film one of the most memorable of its era. Adrian travelled to France, visiting galleries to find original inspiration to enhance his designs and purchasing authentic laces and silks. Back in LA, he put a revolutionary spin on the styling, creating sumptuous replicas of aristocratic draping with a thirties twist. The film is a wonderland of historical detail, and within a few hours I had whipped up some designs and scattered them with hundreds and thousands of tiny Swarovski crystals.

As a designer I have a style and its essence runs from thought to pencil as it moves freely across the page, allowing my imagination to follow. It sometimes moves swiftly and the line is dark and bold, indenting and altering the surface of my paper; often it is faint, more whimsical and indecisive. There is a process to my time spent sketching, and at its best it is comparable to a long walk in the countryside. Firstly, I need to prepare and research – I need to know where I am going – and then I must get into my pace. My first designs are the uneven steps taken finding the path; I waste time retying my boots (finding the right pencil) and then hopefully I switch from consciously walking to striding ahead, fully engaged – sketching. This is the time when the good ideas flow, so I work hard, knowing that sooner or later I will become either lost or tired.

To begin with concentration is crucial, but this quickly gives way to a feeling of relaxation, where I am falling into my work, taking myself into a meditative state by removing myself from everything else. I relish the moment when I can no longer hear the traffic passing outside, when the biscuit tin loses its pull and when the vibrating of my phone doesn't shake me from my thoughts. There is a joy in looking up and realising that you are working in the dark having not noticed the sun slip away, that for a moment you may have forgotten where you are and, on a perfect day, who you are.

I used to plan ahead, engineering days without interruptions, ready with pages of inspiring research, fabric swatches and a peaceful mind, hopeful that my sketching would result in some design brilliance, but I have learnt that comfort and endless time are not prerequisites to producing good work. Michelangelo allegedly worked on his knees, the increasing pain absorbing the temptation to become distracted. Perhaps that is why I design well on a plane and even better on a turbulent one as I use my focus to distract myself from the unnerving bumps, channelling my thoughts into my sketchbook, smoothing the edges of my fear as I scribble. Not exactly the romantic image of the fashion designer sketching surrounded by beautiful fabrics and books, but my life has become a continuous stream of interruptions, so I have adapted: I work quickly in short bursts, speed-sketching.

But, like any artist, I still struggle to settle down in this new world of increasingly wondrous ways to derail the mind. Self-discipline has never felt so tough. And even when the world of modern technology is switched to silent, there sometimes appear to be forces working against me, prising me away from the empty page.

Working from my kitchen table today, I am ready. I have a pot of tea, a few pieces of dark chocolate and four hours of undisturbed time ahead. I will design something wonderful today, I am sure. And then a small mouse runs over my foot, darting towards the wall and disappearing under a kitchen cupboard. I am more annoyed than scared, for as a child it wasn't uncommon for me to pass smooth snakes on the stairs or find frozen birds of prey in the freezer as I rummaged for fishcakes for tea – everyday encounters in the little wildlife reserve that was my home. But then I see another mouse and another, scurrying around the walls, making daring dashes across the tiled open lands, and it dawns on me that it's a big day out for a new family.

I decide to build a humane trap. I empty a small plastic tub and by layering some books I form a flight of stairs, Ziegfeld Follies style. This takes a while as I find one of the books rather interesting – a recently bought biography of Gluck, the gender-bending artist of the thirties. I put some cheese and water into the container, thinking that the mice will climb the stairs and happily jump into the container and that later I will free them onto Hampstead Heath. I ring my brother, who mockingly informs me that, contrary to every cartoon I have ever seen, mice don't eat cheese, and then sends me various internet links to mousetraps. I go online and become absorbed in ways to end my furry infestation, and all the time I am distracting myself – from sketching.

My preoccupation gradually wanes and I return to my work, acknowledging that the mouse problem needs a professional. Resisting the temptation to deflect once more, I begin to draw, gently coaxing myself back into an inspired frame of mind. As the ideas begin to emerge and my pencil begins to chase my thoughts, I become the best part of me. I am the girl sat in her bedroom not wanting to come down for tea, the student working late into the night, and me – the woman, suspended in a beautiful bubble of creativity while on the other side of the room naughty mice in tuxedos with tails and top hats tap dance their way up the stairway to paradise.

Generally, I will be working to design a particular dress for someone, or styles for my latest collection, but at first I always allow myself to draw freely – watching what I draw, observing the direction I have taken. Sketches are beginnings, the workings of the imagination, idle meanderings and sometimes just doodles. They can be something or nothing, treasured or erased. But they are the moment of conception between an almost unconscious collection of creative jumble and structure. And, if I sketch something that sparks excitement in me, I sit back and for a moment imagine I am wearing the dress. I look down, smoothing my hands over my hips, sensing how it feels, questioning the alignment of the seams. I swap shades, visualising the colour against my skin – is it complementary, the best colour for this style? I lower the neckline, plunging it towards my waist, and then pull it up, sensing the tautness of the fabric. I extend the sleeves and play with cuff designs, and gradually, detail by detail, I test-run an invisible design.

To celebrate the end of Dita's European tour I am hosting an intimate supper for her and her London friends and must design her a dress to wear for the evening. I have been thinking about this piece for some time – maybe a little too much – waiting patiently for inspiration to find me. Travelling to the Forbidden City in Beijing earlier in the year, I had hoped to be enthralled by the exquisite workmanship of the gowns of the Emperor's concubines, but this inspiration felt too obvious and so I had filched the colours from the walls of the hidden courtyards and the pillars of the palace's temples. Now, using my imaginary gown simulation technique, I find myself deciding between blood red and imperial blue silk satin, pretending for a moment I have Dita's body! I sketch some 'film noir' silhouettes with wide shoulders, waist-cinching sculpting and splits up each leg, lowering the back neckline to a tantalising level and adding an invisible mesh panel. Among our archive we had found a vintage wallpaper with a print of gradating dots hanging in overlapping loops to give the impression of theatrical curtaining; I use this textile design to lightly cover the transparent mesh in sparkling tonal crystals. I like this stylised reference – the link between the stage drapery of the old-time music hall theatres and Dita's burlesque tour. The reveal-and-conceal characteristics of Dita's style are neatly exposed in this detail.

Nowadays, I don't really like dressing up – is that a terrible thing for me to say? When I do go to a black-tie event and have to make an effort, I do so under duress. The event with Dita is approaching and I am stressing about what to wear. I like to think of myself as a dream maker; my passion is to design for others and perhaps in doing so I am drained of the desire to consider myself. So, I choose to dress in a relatively neutral way so that my designs can take centre stage. I am happy in the shadows while my designs sparkle in the distance, living out my fantasies as they travel the world, dazzling at the best parties and being worn by amazing women. So while for others, I pull out all the stops, the idea of creating a glamorous ensemble for myself holds no interest.

It's the evening of Dita's dinner and I am waiting for her to arrive, along with the other guests, in a cosy hotel bar in Mayfair. I am on my second cocktail and I stop a few sips in, having satisfactorily caught the moment between calming one's nerves and losing the plot. I am told that

Dita has arrived, so I walk to the foyer and watch her pose as the paparazzi stop her in the doorway. Dita is resplendent, the star attraction. The blue sheen of the satin highlights her gentle curves and I congratulate myself on fusing the Ming dynasty with film noir and still managing to throw in a secret nod to the art of striptease. As she turns, the cascading curtain of crystals shimmers against her back, sending a wave of excitement through the room, and I decide to take another sip of my cocktail.

SHAPE

I remember the day Elvis died. It was the day I found my hamster dead behind the washing machine. My parents were out and I laid him on the rug in the dining room, trying to revive him, rubbing his soft ginger fur. Next to him on the floor was the newspaper, ELVIS IS DEAD emblazoned across the front page. I took some bedding from his cage and made a felt-covered pincushion, embroidered 'Hammy' on the top and saddle-stitched the edges. I was ten years old and was contemplating mortality for the first time.

So I'm not sure what I noticed first, the button badge she was wearing – I STILL MISS ELVIS pinned to her lapel – or the woman herself: Magda, a honey blonde in a black suit leaning against the bar. Either way, I quickly recognised that intangible something and made my way over to talk to her. It was late in the evening after a supper party for the make-up artist and businesswoman Bobbi Brown at a vegetarian restaurant in Westbourne Grove – an evening of influencers, brand managers, creatives and lentils. After we had chatted for a while, I told Magda I had to leave and she pulled another Elvis badge from her pocket, gave it to me and told me she was an artist. Magda's version of a glass slipper – or that's how I took it.

Soon after, I asked her if she would collaborate with me. I had just begun working on my 'English Heritage' collection and needed a few quirky ideas for neckerchiefs and scarves. Magda set to work painting corgis, British bulldogs and marching Beefeaters with chunky brushstrokes, adding the twist I was after to the collection – that uniquely British ability to combine wit and style.

One morning, just after we had finished the project, we had breakfast at Chiltern Firehouse and I was invited to visit Magda's wardrobe. I had never received an invitation to a wardrobe before and felt strangely embarrassed, hiding behind my teacup while I thought about how to respond. I had been anticipating an invite to Magda's studio but a combined ticket to the artist's studio and wardrobe was doubly attractive, so I said 'Thank you, I'd like that.'

But it was not an arbitrary suggestion. Magda and I can sustain a conversation about our sartorial adventures for an outstandingly long time. It starts as soon as we see each other. Like most women, our warm-up act is an exchange of compliments about what we are wearing – 'You look great. I love that shirt'. Then the story behind the purchase unfolds, there is a quick recap of its provenance, how it was altered (we both tend to remodel our purchases), and then we zoom in on the details, the colour, cut and maybe even the price. As the fashion chat falls away the catch-up begins: work, home, husbands, some gossip, a little problem-solving and then perhaps an upcoming event will be mentioned and I'll say 'What are you going to wear?' And we are back, divulging our aspirations and current well-being through the language of fashion.

Often she will bring me a gift, something that will inspire me: an original scrapbook of royal clippings – a collection of meticulously glued, faded fashion moments from the 1940s featuring the Queen and Princess Margaret in Hartnell, shot by Beaton, on tour and at home. Last time we met she pulled from her bag a swatch of gold lurex pinned to a piece of blue ribbon. 'Can you make me something like that?' she asked, and I looked at the fabrics in my hand and was reminded of the Queen and her love of gold lurex and a blue swishy sash – very much like the colour of the ribbon I was holding – and I wondered if Magda was after something majestic.

I like Magda's style, but how would I describe it? She has that Los Angeles art scene (circa 1980s) way of wearing colour-popping details, and in the same way that David Hockney, the West Coast's king of 'goofy' cool, would appear to have toppled out of one of his paintings, Magda's personal style and her work are a homogeneous blend.

For me, Magda's saccharine painting *My Life is Crap*, reminiscent of a 1960s greeting card, encapsulates her painting style. A cartoonish lamb with smiling eyes kicks up its hind legs in playful joy, frolicking on a bed of daffodils and tulips while the slogan My Life is Crap dances around it. Initially the image evokes happiness. The colours are attractive – pretty pastels with dabs of fluoro-pink and lime – but then the irony of the painting's slogan sinks in. This juxtaposition conveys one of the realities of modern life: that perhaps we are not as happy with our lives as we appear.

In the same way, Magda's everyday fashion style is often punctuated with a detail – a badge or a hand-painted statement across the back of a leather jacket – that will make you stop and think. Magda's style is not flippant, and her messages, which are often anti-establishment or sensitive, are unexpected and therefore more provocative. Her connection to fashion is intrinsically artistic and, like with many creative people, the evolution of a strong, recognisable personal style can be an important component of both the artist's success and legacy.

There is a close relationship between art and fashion, but whether fashion is art has been a hot topic for a while. The question of what makes one form of creative output more 'art' than another has no definitive answer, although one might suggest that art should have some value from a historical perspective. Our clothes, like art, are a means of self-expression, and what we choose to wear reflects our cultural, psychological and political inclinations. They become a visual manifestation not just of us, but of our time and, therefore, in my opinion, should be considered art.

The flow of inspiration from an artist's work to their appearance can produce a unique sartorial aesthetic. Georgia O' Keeffe, Frida Kahlo, David Hockney, Tracey Emin – even Vincent Van Gogh – are such connoisseurs of this that their wardrobes have become synonymous with their work. Imagine for a moment that, instead of donning androgynous elegant tailoring, O'Keeffe had flipped her fashion style as regularly as other women born in the late 1800s (from Victorian corsetry, to flapper girl, to the wasp-waisted New Look of the fifties) and rather than wearing monochrome shades, she had changed her colours every season. O'Keeffe's personal style is ever-present when we view her work. The artist and her considered sense of fashion have been immortalised in iconic portraits, beautifully minimalistic black and white images by her husband, the photographer Alfred Stieglitz, complementing her work's sensuality by their powerful simplicity.

Meanwhile, Emin admits to preferring to paint naked – a revealing insight that enforces the bare-all nature of her work. The absence of 'a wardrobe' gives the impression that Emin's work is pure expression, raw and honest. And her 'dressed' style, often a bust-cinching Vivienne Westwood design worn with high heels, is rebellious by association. All of which creates integrity around her work.

Let's get back to Magda. I arrive at her house late in the afternoon and we go straight to her studio, which takes up an entire side of the first floor of her double-fronted house, and then she disappears to get us some tea. As I wait, I look around. At either end of the room are high sash windows that let in a warm golden glow of light. Everything is painted white, and the walls, which are covered with floor-to-ceiling shelving, are crammed with 'stuff', colourful and very attractive stuff that I want to pick up and look at: collected memorabilia arranged on untidily stacked books, cute pre-loved furry toys and reclaimed gifts, vintage ornaments, tourist treasures and snow globes. A plastic Charlie Brown snuggles up to a statue of the Virgin Mary and a toy

Dumbo appears to be licking the ear of a sculpture of JFK, icons of popular culture playfully interacting. Each shelf is edged by pinned-up postcards and photographs and there is so much 'clobber' (a word my father would use that somehow seems appropriate) that I can't seem to focus on anything. I look down; paintings, prints and guitars are propped up against the walls, every available surface is covered with bright and interesting things.

Magda returns with the tea and I give her a ceramic ornament of a small bird that I found in a gift shop in Istanbul. She says 'Thanks, I'll put it on my bird shelf' and, as she does, I scan the room again and realise that there is an order to this beautiful mess. Noddy is not alone and a dozen coy Snow Whites in matching dresses and head-bands are eyeing up each other's twist on fairy-tale fashion, while beside them a crowd of Grumpys, Happys and Dopeys are gathered. On the shelf below, a small pack of sculptured miniature terriers are lined up nose to tail, sniffing.

After a quick tour of the studio and a preview of Magda's latest work in progress, we go upstairs. In her bedroom, I take a seat at her dressing table and open my sketchbook to make notes. As Magda opens the doors to her wardrobe and I peek inside, it is as if bubbles and brightly coloured balloons float out into the bedroom and streamers come tumbling out of the half-opened shoeboxes. And if there were to be an accompanying soundtrack it would be my childhood memory of the sound of the ice cream van approaching from a few streets away, the prelude to a treat. In other words, there seems to be a party going on in Magda's wardrobe.

'Style makes people want to look. I always go in for a second look when I see it,' Magda said recently when I asked her how she would describe 'style'. And as the contents of her wardrobe, popping with colour and print, spill out into the daylight, I go in to look more closely.

Polka dots, stripes and printed pretty scarlet hearts jostle for my attention and, in the same way her studio initially appeared chaotic, the liveliness of the clothes sends me into a bit of a spin. My instinct is to touch, to run my hand over the fabrics, pulling out the styles for a closer look. But I'm not in a vintage shop – I can't even buy anything, I'm just looking.

Magda's choice of colour is consistent with her paintings and the eclectic interior of her studio. 'Pure pigment dressing' (straight out of the tube) is Magda's description of her rainbow palette of primary shades, touches of fluorescent and dashes of hot bright pink and sunshine yellow. And her playful selection of prints is 'conversational'. This is one of my favourite fashion expressions and a term given to textile prints that are – literally – something to talk about. There is usually a theme – a rocket blasting into space, an Edwardian picnic scene or an illustrated map of Paris – and although Magda's clothing is not gimmicky, a dress covered with lipstick kisses or dotted with flamingos would present an opportunity to chat.

JP: How do you choose what you wear? Is it an emotional decision or do you consciously create a look?

MA: I like references. I think about what to wear more than I probably should, but I enjoy it, looking at books and images. I've always liked that blonde Californian thing, that laid-back beach style, tanned and golden, not a care in the world – Farrah Fawcett on a skateboard! All those Charlie perfume ads with Shelley Hack – looking fly and sassy in a trouser suit, Margaux Hemingway in the Babe advert or Catherine Deneuve in her YSL with a tan and that gorgeous hair, wearing flared jeans in the South of France. Bianca Jagger, Cybill Shepherd, Jane Birkin, Britt Ekland always looking lovely. My all-time favourite dress-ers are Debbie Harry, Linda McCartney, Farrah, Carolyn Bessette-Kennedy – I loved her …

During our conversation Magda has been pulling out styles, and in the same way her studio is arranged by genre, her wardrobe is organised into blouses, dresses, jackets. There is definitely a seventies theme, and many of the dresses are similar in silhouette and design, a plunging V neckline with a waistband and interesting sleeves. There is a mixture of vintage and contemporary finds and the vivid colours and prints give each style individuality. This is a wardrobe of 'one-offs' rather than a coordinated selection to mix and match, and I get the feeling that Magda has a connection with each piece, either by way of a memory or an attachment to a design detail.

JP: How do you plan for a special event? Do you go shopping?

MA: No, not shopping – I hate trawling! I look at what I already have and put things together. I have a lady who alters and remakes my clothes – I might ask her to reshape something. I find it hard not to change things. Nothing is ever 'quite right' but I still buy it. I'll choose it for its print or colour. Frances, who alters my clothes, is a costume designer for TV and film. She understands me, what I'm getting at and the look I'm after. Often this is a cross between a 1940s and 1970s vibe.

JP: Do you care what others think about what you wear?

MA: No, it doesn't matter to me what others think.

JP: I don't believe you ... but OK. What do you feel most comfortable in, a suit or a dress?

MA: It used to be a suit but now I find you can get more life out of a dress. I mix things up with the shoes. I often wear 1970s-style platform sandals, my perfect shoes! My mum refused to buy me a pair of shoes in the late seventies; they were blue with a red stitched-on apple motif ... I'd love a pair today. And please don't get me started on the red cork wedges that a friend 'borrowed' from her au pair to lend to me to wear to a school disco ... I HAVE DREAMS ABOUT THOSE SHOES, I've been obsessed with red shoes and sandals ever since.

I'm very partial to a scarf and adding a pop of colour. I do like shoes or boots which have studs on them, but as far as clothes go I like specific colour combinations. Some remind me of clothing I've owned in the past and others of clothing my family or friends had, some of the clothes I wanted but did not get.

JP: Some of the prints in your wardrobe remind me of things from when I was young – is it the same for you?

MA: Yes, I LOVE an evocative print. Gingham reminds me of my childhood. I remember I had a black and white gingham shirt. One of my sisters had a green and white one and the other one (sister) had a blue and white one. Of course, I wanted that one so now I'm a sucker for anything in blue and white gingham. I'm very partial to clothes with a cherry print and I LOVE polka dots. They're breezy and cheerful. My mum made me a lot of my clothes and my sisters grew out of things, which I inherited. Later on, I 'stole' things from my dad's wardrobe – he had a nice denim jacket and a beautiful cashmere jumper. He instilled in me a love of stripy T-shirts. I started buying a lot of second-hand stuff in my teens and twenties – partly because I didn't have any money but also because I thought it was treasure.

JP: Do you think that the way you dress reflects your personality, truthfully?

MA: Yes.

JP: And does it reflect your art? Is it important that it does?

MA: I don't think it's important that my clothes reflect my art, why should it matter? But I like the way that some artists dress. Pablo Picasso was a knockout dresser, but now David Hockney is king, for sure, then there's Humphrey Ocean, Peter Blake in his double denim customised with badges, Grayson Perry, and Jenny Saville has something special. Damien has that rock star thing going on. Antony Gormley has a vibe. And then Jeff Koons; I'm interested in how Jeff's progressed from the snow-washed jeans, sweatshirt and 'dad trainers' into the perfect suit and white shirt … I'd like to see him in the eighties get-up again. I like Rose Wylie in her high-tops, jumper and skirt combo, the list goes on …

JP: So, what's your favourite colour? I always love the childishness of that question.

MA: I have colour crushes. I love fluoro-pink, process yellow, emerald green, cobalt blue, and there are colour combinations I love: pink and khaki, yellow and blue, pink and red, gold and blue … orange and grey … I just love colour but I do wear a lot of white; my most comfortable look at the moment is white trousers and T-shirt with a bright, fluorescent scarf, but I also wear white when I feel vulnerable. It's my opting-out look; there are no complications, I don't have to think about colour.

JP: That's funny, I feel really uncomfortable in white. If I put a white shirt on, I spend all day just wanting to take it off. If I am actually feeling 'vulnerable' I just want to cover myself, I want that feeling of being under the bedcovers but still walking about, so I wear layers – jumpers, scarves …

MA: I suppose I want to look like a patient – but a patient that is not ill.

Magda continues to talk. She is saying something about buying things she likes in two colours, but I'm not really listening, I am thinking about what she has just said about wearing white and now my mind is releasing flickering images of 'asylum wear' in the movies – *One Flew Over the Cuckoo's Nest*; *Girl, Interrupted*; *Shutter Island*. This is interfering with what I'm really trying to understand: why would Magda want to look like a patient? Her wardrobe is so 'up' – bright and inspiring, bursting with a sense of love and optimism for life – so her remark got me thinking about the lamb painting and the fact that we all feel vulnerable sometimes. Magda's wardrobe reflects not only her use of colour but also the emotional impulses that translate through into her work.

Magda's comment also helps to explain the embarrassment I felt when the idea of looking into her wardrobe was first mentioned – there is something rather intimate about delving into someone else's closet.

I think of my own. It's not quite what I would have imagined it to be at my age – it's still very much a work in progress. And like most women I recognise the mistakes, regrets, shameful expenditures and hopeful purchases, and the garments waiting for the moment that may never come. But it's not a sad place; I can see that I'm busy, serious and intent on evolving, a pragmatic person who occasionally gets carried away – a bit impulsive but not reckless. I can let go of the past, I'm not a hoarder and I'm not fighting with my changing body shape or age – I don't bear grudges. And there are, unsurprisingly, some sparkly things hanging on my rail: glamorous black slinky satin palazzo pants, sharp-shouldered jackets with crystal embellishment and trainers decorated with sequins. But if I were a wardrobe therapist, I would suggest I needed to give myself more time, stop being so sensible and 'lighten up'.

JP: So, Magda, what would you grab from your wardrobe if you had to leave quickly? Just a few items?

MA: My 'yard sale' jeans, a white T-shirt and a scarf. What about you?

JP: Mmm ... Maybe I'd grab a few of the clothes I have yet to wear ...

*

'This is my special underpants drawer,' Chris says, as he pulls out a pair of outrageous designer leopard-print shorts. He likes to walk about in his pants at home and I've seen these before, when he stayed overnight recently. Usually, I don't look at my brother's bottom, but it had been impossible not to. Lime and tan with jagged black spots and a silhouette of a growling black leopard on one side, these cocky pants were made to be looked at.

My brother is Chris Packham the TV presenter, naturalist, writer, photographer, conservationist, campaigner and film-maker. He also has Asperger's – an autistic disorder that causes challenges with social interaction and non-verbal communication, along with restricted and repetitive behaviour and interest. Growing up, his own high-performing version of this condition wound the most wondrous web around my childhood years, and his dedication to propelling his thoughts into reality created a family life devoid of dullness. While he spun like a Catherine wheel firing off flickering sparks of magic, we stood close by, lit up by his excitement. For my parents, there was no condition, and for me, well, he was my hero.

Meanwhile, for Chris, my mum and dad were the catering and transport and I was the annoying sister who threw up in the car on the long journeys to see 'boring birds' and wanted the loo at the very moment we arrived at his treasure of choice at the Natural History Museum.

Sometimes when he was out in the garden or the woods, I would give his bedroom a 'clean'. This gave me a justifiable reason to trespass. I would pull out his drawer of precious eggshells that lay neatly on a bed of cotton wool and run my finger gently over their fragile speckled surfaces, admiring their delicate shades and perfect symmetry. And in his box of feathers, 'downy', 'tail' and 'flight' were separated and laid together. I would take one out, gently pulling apart the barbs and tickling my nose with its delicate plumage. But as I dutifully dusted Chris's room, I would have my sights on the small wooden cupboard above the sink. This is where he kept the leather jesses, leashes and embroidered hoods, the falconry paraphernalia for his kestrel, and this was always my favourite place to clean. Inside the cabinet, the stylish Indian imports laced with tiny bells and intricately stitched skins appeared to me like an exclusive, miniature wardrobe of designer wear for raptors.

His wardrobe had a forward-facing rail that extended out into the bedroom. An inherited piece of bulky 1940s furniture, in which I would occasionally be sent to hide when he wanted to play detectives. We had a secret sign to initiate this game. While watching television with our parents, he would attract my attention and then quickly look away, rubbing his index finger upwards on the side of his nose. My mission was to go upstairs, conceal myself in his bedroom and wait. Crouched in the armoire with his shirt cuffs brushing the top of my head, I would listen for his footsteps on the stairs, terrified. Then, by peeking through a gap, I would catch sight of his shadow as he shimmied around the open door and into the room, disappearing into the darkness. After creeping about for a few interminable minutes, he would suddenly fling open the door and yell at me in a French accent, causing me to jump out of the wardrobe and onto the floor, where he would tickle me to death. I think he got the idea from the Pink Panther movies; he was Inspector Clouseau and I was Cato – except he always won.

But today there is nowhere to hide. The lights are on and the only thing that frightens me is that Chris seems intent on showing me the entirety of his wardrobe – starting with his pants and a collection of black woollen socks. I'm upstairs in Chris's home, a secluded cottage in a dreamy location in ancient woodland in the New Forest, Hampshire. It is picturesque, quaint and quintessentially English, with wooden beams and inglenook fireplaces. But Chris is no country bumpkin, and the interior is quite a contrast to the cottage's postcard-perfect architecture. Sleek, modern furniture and wall-to-wall art create a vibrant atmosphere and reflect the diversity of his passions – a devotion to the natural world and a love of art and design.

You don't have a lot of underpants, do you? I say, teasing him.

'No. I only showed you my special underpants – the ones I don't wear much,' he replies. 'I've got several different types. I've got flying underpants – the ones I wear when I fly because they are really comfortable; I've got daily underpants, and then I've got ones that I should actually throw away because they are a bit raggedy, the ones you don't want to die in.' He laughs.

I'm really not that interested in his pants, but his seriousness is endearing, and this detailed explanation is typical of
his approach to almost everything in his life. With Chris,
nothing is ever imprecise.

How many pairs have you got, then?

'Once a year I go to Selfridges and buy about eight new
pairs, so I've probably got about twenty, but they are in
three groups, and then on top of that I've got walking-the-
dog ones.'

In his bedroom there are a few drawers for his 'smalls',
one for his speciality socks, another for ties, thermals, tops,
and a few cupboards for shoes, which are arranged side by
side, polished up, with immaculately clean soles. Most of
his wardrobe is in two adjoining rooms that take up almost
the entirety of the top floor of the cottage. Apart from a
double-sided fitted wardrobe, where he keeps his shirts
and long-sleeved T-shirts, Chris's clothes are arranged on
hanging rails, and at first it feels a bit like a mini department store. There are different categories: outdoor wear,
T-shirts, coats, jackets and trousers, and subgroups
arranged by designer, style and colour. The outdoor collection is spread over at least three rails. This is the technical
stuff, the Gore-Tex weatherproof jackets for his sub-zero
trips to Antarctica, and his *Autumnwatch* fleecy layers dis-
played in graduating earthy shades. The hangers are equally

spaced, and while we talk he keeps adjusting them, edging them back and forward until they are perfectly equidistant. Tidiness and organisation are essential to Chris, and his wardrobe is magnificent in its order and immaculate lay-out. Perhaps if he wasn't my brother I might be worried about him, but I have come to understand his need to control his environment. It's not OCD – it's just the way he likes it.

I want to know about his working wardrobe, so I ask him to describe how he chooses what he wears on television and how it differs from the rest of his wardrobe.

'It is completely different. It has to be practical and I need to buy multiples of it. It needs to be durable and wash-able. The only time I wear more of my own style is during *Springwatch*. So aside from that I just dress practically because a lot of the time I'm going to be wet, I'm going to be snowed on or I'm going to be hot. So I have to choose clothes that are not going to show all the sweat, clothes that I know I can wash wherever I am because I only have three of them – I get three of anything I wear on TV. It's not about looking good, it's about looking the same.'

This isn't the truth. Chris's love of designer wear is well known, and to pretend that his sartorial selection for his screen time is purely practical makes me smile. Chris must be responsible for introducing Prada to some of the most remote peoples in the world, and I imagine the Galapagos mockingbird is still tweeting about sighting Chris's new Louis Vuitton raincoat.

Chris's wardrobe is also a bit like a Prada outlet shop, and I ask him to explain his long-standing loyalty to the brand.

'I like the way it's clean and simple – simple cuts,' he says, pulling out a Prada shirt. 'Look, it's black and white and it's got the one little red line on it.' It sounds like he's talking about a great spotted woodpecker rather than a shirt – but maybe that's why he likes it so much.

'There is always something a little bit obtuse about Prada's designs,' he continues. 'More recently it's been the colours they've used – they are quite different. It is also about convenience – Prada suits me and I like the shops.'

So how do you like to feel in clothes? What's important to you when you choose what to wear?

'Just that I'm smart, neat, tidy – I think that's it. But things have changed. I think you have to be aware of your age. I was shopping this week and there are a lot of things I like but I couldn't wear them any longer because, basically, I mean, I could if I was thirty but I'm fifty-nine and I can't.'

My mind goes back to the audacious underpants, and I try to think of another question to shift the image, so I ask him about the hangers.

'I just like everything in order, everything catalogued,' he replies. 'Believe it or not, there is a catalogue going on here.'

Yes, but *why* is it so important that it's all so tidy? I ask.

'It's about controlling my space. I can't control that space out there (the world), and I struggle with lots of it. In here, I have the capacity to control my space. So this is the extreme example of that. This is about me saying, I want these hangers lined up like this because I think it's neat and tidy. And I like the cataloguing.'

But what if you thought differently – that there was a kind of beauty in having different spacing between—

'No,' he interrupts. 'There's not.'

Not even in an artistic way?

'No.' He laughs.

Because they're not exactly the same distance away from each other, are they Chris? (I can't help myself.)

'No. But, they're close enough for it to be tolerable.'

Could you not find pleasure in a bit of hanger chaos?

'No!' he says, having the final word.

Chris has been a stickler for style for as long as I can remember. When we were young, there would always be a particular item he was yearning for – a Brutus collared shirt, a pair of pea-green Marc Bolan-style high-waisted

Oxford bags, a Starsky (and Hutch) blue and cream wrapover cardigan (my mum's greatest knitting moment). The wish-list was family knowledge, and in the same way that we were all poised to enable a sudden journey – a birder's tip-off that would send us out into the countryside to get a 'twitcher's tick' on his list of birds to see – we were also poised to assist in the hunt for or creation of his sartorial obsessions.

So, in February 1987, Chris and I got the cross-Channel ferry from Portsmouth on a cheap Valentine's Special three-day all-inclusive coach tour to Paris. It was a night-time crossing and, unable to sleep in the seats provided, we found ourselves rolling with the swell of the Channel across the deck – seasick and uncomfortable. In Paris the next morning, we left the rest of our group at the hotel, bypassing the city's sights to find our way to the newly opened Jean Paul Gaultier shop (the purpose of the trip), where Chris spent a small fortune on a black wool coat edged with tape embroidered with 'Gaultier' translated into Russian. To celebrate, we ordered champagne in Philippe Starck's uppish Café Costes and later that night had an impromptu photo shoot, with Chris posing in his new coat at the top of the Eiffel Tower, the world at our feet. The next evening as we boarded the coach to return home, the other passengers looked on with suspicion as the strange Béatrice Dalle and

Billy Idol lookalikes made their way to the back of the bus and slept. But perhaps my favourite memory of this adventure in fashion is Chris and me pushing our baggage home in a rather wayward Safeway supermarket trolley in the early hours of the morning – laughing hysterically as the trolley hit the kerb again and again.

So, do you keep things that are memorable to you? I ask.

'Always,' he says. 'Out in the garage, I've got all my clothes. I've got that Gaultier coat.'

What about the suit you wore to the palace to get your CBE? Would that be something you keep?

'No.'

But you do keep things that are memorable to you?

'Yeah, I do.'

I ask Chris about the importance of feeling confident in his clothes and how this affects his work – in particular his campaigning on environmental and wildlife issues.

'I think because of the Asperger's thing, it's always about confidence. I only pick a fight knowing that I've got enough information to prove that I'm right and I have to be able to present myself and to be judged. And people are constantly judging me for what I say, and ultimately the way I look. And the way I look is mostly what I'm wearing. Therefore, I have to be confident in what I'm wearing. It's about making me feel good. And that's more important because then what comes out of me – my words – is more likely to be successful. So, it's less about me thinking, "Well, if I wear this, I'll get a good reaction." It's about, "If I wear this, I'll feel good and then I'll be able to elicit a good reaction." So, it's more about the way I feel in those clothes.

'And a lot of these clothes in my wardrobe are empowering. When I wear my slogan T-shirts, particularly if they're ones I designed myself, then that is tremendously empowering. I've come up with a message and a design that I believe in and I put it on my chest.'

It's getting late and Chris's young poodles, Sid and Nancy, are yapping downstairs, bored with having to play without their pack leader, and I need to get back to London. But we don't really want to stop. We don't get much time together and his wardrobe is providing us with an enjoyable means to communicate about our lives. Every garment he wants to talk about seems to take the discussion somewhere new.

Prompted by the barking, Chris wants to show me his indoor clothes, and from a neat pile in the corner of the room he holds up a sweatshirt printed with a life-size photographic image of Neil Armstrong's spacesuit.

'When I come in, I put on the same clothes every day. This is the top I wear at the moment – and I wear these trousers,' he says, showing me some jogging pants. 'Because the thing about my dogs is that when I come in and I put my indoor clothes on, they know that I'm not going out so they go mad – they go berserk and I love that.'

I didn't know about this phenomenon, and I wonder whether my dog recognises that when I come in and go upstairs and take off my bra after work it means that I'm definitely not going out. I make a mental note to look out for an increase in tail-wagging.

'Chris,' I say, trying to get his attention as he refolds his indoor clothes. 'This is my last question: tell me what you have in your wardrobe that takes you back to your childhood.'

'I like the sort of Captain Scarlett look,' he says without pausing to think. 'So when I wear my things, I always wear them like him, with my top button done up. I can't stand anything undone. I like those uniforms from *Thunderbirds*, I mean they had a massive impact on me. I've got loads of stuff like that.'

And what about Dad? Dad was always really smart; appearance is very important to him, being neat and tidy. And he likes to wear very similar jumpers to you – the cardigans with the zipped-up front. He likes that high-neck thing. How much influence do you think Dad had on your sartorial choices?

'None,' he replies.

That's not true.

'Do you want to see my mountaineering gear?' he asks, abruptly changing the subject. 'And if you say I dress anything like Dad, I'll sue you,' he adds, smirking.

And with that I am transported back in time. It's Sunday lunchtime and we are all sitting at the dining room table, Mum, Dad, Chris and me. I think he is about 22 and I am 18. It's autumn, a bit cloudy, and everything seems normal until I see a small wisp of smoke floating towards the window and the faint smell of kindling hits the back of my throat. My dad is the last one to look out into the back garden and it is my mum's sharp intake of breath followed by my brother's sudden wicked burst of laughter that shifts his gaze out towards the lawn, where my dad's favourite cardigan – the one with a zip and a high neck – is hung on a wooden cross, flames darting up towards its ribbed hem, burning at the stake.

I wonder. Was Chris's ritual incineration of my dad's jumper symbolic of the transference of power – of the right to wear the zip-up cardigan – from father to son? After all, there can only be one Captain Scarlett on Planet Earth.

However, on reflection, it does seem to me that Chris's wardrobe, rather than a collection of emotional decisions, *is* practical, and motivated largely, as he says, by the need to appear and feel in control of life. I didn't ask Chris what he wears when he feels vulnerable. I can predict the puzzled look on his face and anyway, do I really want to know? But if I had to guess, I think it would be his Neil Armstrong sweatshirt. Maybe on a bad day he lies on the floor in his cottage, closes his eyes and listens for the build-up of thrust, the fierce rumble of the engines and the jolt of the swing arms falling away from the launch tower as the propulsion of *Saturn V* slingshots him into space. Entering Earth's orbit, the engines are cut and he looks down at our world, a little vulnerable blue dot, exploring its surface in detail, entranced by the profundity of the view. Then his need to try to protect our planet, to rebel against our extinction, would kick in and he would come home.

EMBELLISHMENT

I'm not a minimalist designer, no one would say that. Embellishment has been an integral part of my creativity for three decades and is in the brand's DNA. Looking back to when I started designing, I think I knew I had to find a way to get my work noticed, and so I began experimenting with texture. This attention-seeking ploy worked and I was hooked. I like classic, flattering shapes; I don't try to change the silhouette of the female body because I like it the way it is. But by adding beadwork, embroidery and prints, I have been able to offer uniqueness in my work. When I started designing professionally, I found my resources in London were limited and I struggled to make the clothes I dreamt of. So, as soon as we had the funds to travel, we did, searching out experts in China and India. These early trips to the other side of the world opened up exciting new possibilities for surface design and transformed my collections.

It's 6am and I'm on the Heathrow Express to Terminal 5. I haven't spoken yet, it was a late night and I am on auto-pilot. I stare at the BBC newsfeed on the elevated screen in front of me and as the bulletin ends a new clip begins. We are in Jerusalem and a bearded man with a long white stick is crossing a street. He is blind and I watch as the camera follows him towards the Wailing Wall. He is swiping the stick from side to side, clearing a route for himself, and then he arrives, reaching out gently, exploring the wall's craggy surface, running his fingers, as if reading Braille, over the folded prayers wedged between the ancient stones. I have no idea what he is experiencing but I try to imagine what it must be like to be so dependent on touch.

I sigh as I reflect on my thoughts earlier that morning. When the alarm woke me, I had buried my head in the pillow as the tiring realisation that tonight I would be in bed somewhere in New Delhi sank in. I was exhausted and I lay there inventing get-out plans. I glance at the TV screen again; the clip is ending and the man is walking into the distance, continuing his journey around the world. His determination to travel despite his disabilities instantly dissolves my self-pity and vivid memories of India come flooding back and I begin to feel excitement. Beautiful colours come swirling into frame, provoking remembered

Glamour
★
STRONG, CONFIDENT
Beauty
★
WALK LIKE A
MOVIE STAR!
(STEADY PACE, SEXY)
~ MARILYN

glimpses of fuchsia, emerald and amber silks scattered with golden paisleys, and as I pick up scents of sandalwood and jasmine I recapture the clichéd snapshots of mountains of burnt-orange turmeric on street stalls and handfuls of brightly coloured beads.

My love of travelling is no secret and I am indebted to my ancestors for my itchy feet. My grandfather Harold was an able seaman and most notably accompanied Sir Malcolm Campbell to the Cocos Islands in search of hidden treasure. In 1933, at the height of the depression, Harold, newly married and with my father barely a year old, took ill-advised employment on a coaster delivering coal around the east coast of England. Tragically, he was swallowed by the sea along with eight others as a storm hit the overloaded and shoddy boat and it floundered a mile offshore near Aldeburgh. Despite this family tragedy, my father, Colin, became an officer in the Merchant Navy, getting grimy down in the engine room during the day and scrubbing up for shore leave in order to bring home tales to last a lifetime. However, after five years, marriage brought him home and tethered him to a job as a marine engineer for a company in Southampton designing and selling galley equipment for boats. His lust for travel endured and, while my mum berated him for leaving us, I waited patiently for his stories and gifts from foreign lands – beyond the end of the road.

As kids we never had holidays; when we did leave home it was to join my dad on business trips to Scotland aboard the HMS Austin Maxi, following him from port to port, and impatiently waiting in shoreline car parks as he climbed onto shipping boats or into Portakabins to 'leave a brochure and show his face'. Meanwhile, my brother and I sat in the back seat with our polo-necked jumpers rolled up over our noses while my mum rolled down the windows to let in the unforgettable fragrance of *Eau de Cod* – the scent of freshly caught fish being unloaded from the previous night's trawl. When my dad returned, we would drive into the Scottish countryside on a mission to track down otters and golden eagles to quell my brother's obsessional desire to see these particularly elusive species. With our noses pinned to the windows, we would be caught up in his search, flipping our gaze between the streams and the tree-tops in the hope of catching a glimpse and ending the hunt.

My treat would be a visit to a Highland gift shop, where I would caress the wobbly stacks of tartan scarves, memorising their clan names and checking out their wool content. I would try on kilts and wrap myself in mohair shawls, cat-walking between the aisles of Aran sweaters and sheepskin rugs as my parents debated whether to get the shortbread or the butter fudge, oblivious to my 'Flora MacDonald spring/summer 1975' collection.

When Chris and I were older, my mum dared to leave us when she accompanied Dad on his trips. On their return, she would announce that there would be a Sunday-evening slide show in the back room. The dining chairs would be arranged into rows, and only close neighbours and best friends would be invited. After attaching a bedsheet to the nets to create a blackout effect, she would flick through her famously out-of-focus frames as we followed her through the markets of Hong Kong and into Egyptian tombs while my dad passed round the ham sandwiches. We would sit in the back row (the one behind the first row) giggling and making disparaging comments about her photographic efforts – like teenagers do. Later in her life, she would announce that she was 'off to see the snow' or 'going West' and catch a coach from the pub up the road and be gone.

As a family we never seem truly settled and consider travelling the quickest way to escape ordinariness. However, holidays are deemed questionable wastes of money, indulgent and pointless. Within the Packham family, the idea of investing in a week spent idly relaxing is appalling. Travel is for exploring and, for those of us lucky enough, a 'work trip' is the approved mode of transport.

*

My mission in India is to work closely with the artisans who translate our drawings into creative embroideries, and use their inherited craftmanship to enrich our collection. I will see the styles in progress and make changes, tweaking and tampering, pulling the work back from artistic indulgence and into desirable garments. I am in my element during these visits, away from the daily digressions of my life. My imagination bubbles, and I hurry back to my hotel room eager to sketch up new ideas. While some designers may grow weary of returning to the source, my passion for connecting with my product, catching it in construction, has never waned. In London, with folders of sample sequins, beads and crystals, my team plot the patterned landscape of a style and, using our combined imaginations, we visualise the outcome of our work. However, in reality and 4,000 miles away, a dyed fabric can slip a shade, batches of coded sequins can fade with time and sometimes carefully matched colours and textures can lose their balance.

So I stand over the beading frames embarrassed by my lust for perfection and ask the artisans to remove lines of perfect stitching so that I can try something new. They oblige without complaint. Over the years I have learnt that if I see a potential calamity before me, I must stop the work and suffer the groans of a tired team. To allow work on a style to continue when it is clear things have strayed is time and money. So, when I need to, I hesitate and determine whether to go forward, to redesign or quietly send a style into the cupboard of forgotten gowns. This is why my trip is so important. As a design evolves, each process needs attention, and it is the constant dialogue of the team that will ensure its success. To create a good dress, you must closely follow its path or, like Chinese whispers, it can mutate into an unexpected version of itself, sometimes good, but mostly not.

In Delhi, I stay at the Imperial Hotel. The car bringing me from the airport sweeps into the hotel's palm-lined driveway and the colonial elegance of this art deco master-piece is a shocking contrast to the ramshackle buildings lining the streets from the airport. Distinguished-looking doormen in swishy uniforms topped with turbans welcome me into the luxurious interior – a decadent throwback to the days of the Raj. The hotel was built in 1934 by F.B. Blom-field, an associate of Edwin Lutyens, and was the hang-out for the British and Indian elite. A place to play croquet and have a pot of Twinings tea while the powerful planned the partition of India in the hotel bar. Its corridors are laden with colonial art and, after dinner, I roam them counting dead tigers, trophies of the barbaric hunts of yesteryear. But despite this, I fall for the hotel's style and languish in its old-world glamour.

Early the next morning I visit our factory in Delhi, excited to see some special pieces in progress. I must admit that creating embroidered dresses for an Indian clientele does seem like selling pizzas to Italians, so I was surprised recently when an eminent Indian family requested an appointment in our London store to shop for an upcoming family wedding. They ordered, and my plan is to deliver the dresses when I reach Mumbai in a week's time. At the factory I am given a swatch of one of the styles, a small piece of fabric on which a few lines of beading have been sewn. A beaded gown can take 275 hours for one embroiderer to complete, and on this particular style I estimate there are at least 70,000 3mm sequins to apply in a linear design, edge to edge and slightly overlapping, to cover the entire surface of the dress. It is obvious the order has not been started, and the family's PA has been texting me for an update since I arrived. I am beginning to feel anxious.

I should be used to this by now. There are always deadlines: weddings, red-carpet moments, diplomatic receptions. Everything must be perfect and on time – I am rarely granted a second chance; so I take a moment to decide my next steps.

Fortunately, the family have celebrity status in India and the factory's attachment to fame will endorse the quality of their work; so they are motivated to complete the gowns, and even offer to carry them by hand to Mumbai if necessary. Sometimes it's the challenge of these projects, the seemingly impossible turnaround time, that ignites our passion, driving us to deliver. Fast-tracking dresses requires international teamwork. We push the 'emergency gown' button and start couriering beads, fabrics and trims across continents and receiving images of the work in progress. While the client books her hairstylist and self-tans, her dress is flying around the world, being embellished into the night by artisans and stitched frantically together in our studio.

I decide to take a break from anxiously hovering about in the factory and check out of the Imperial. Early the next day, I find myself in the Palace Square at Amer Fort, an ancient tourist attraction on the outskirts of Jaipur. Tales of the Pink City's shopping arcades flowing with textural delights, whispers of royal palaces with mirrored ceilings and galleries of vintage clothing gathered from the Maharaja's closets have pulled me to this place. However, I am late to the party and, as I tour the must-see sights of this vibrant town, I know I am merely following in my contemporaries' footsteps. Other designers have already ravaged the inspirational highlights and pilfered its exotic essence for their own collections. I wonder if there is anything left for me to take.

I find a bench to sit on in the corner of the square and take out my sketchbook. A few days earlier I had trudged through the woodland of Hampstead Heath with my dog. A recent storm had blown the leaves from the trees to form a mushy mattress underfoot and the autumn crispness had given way to a wintery bite, so I had curtailed our walk and headed home. So I take a moment to appreciate the warming of my skin and close my eyes, enjoying the golden rays of this Indian summer.

A crowd of teenage girls pass by, chattering and laughing, seemingly oblivious to the UNESCO-blessed architecture of the red sandstone courtyard while they meander across to the shady central pavilion. The guidebook informs me that the square was originally a place for the Maharanis, the queens, and their female entourage to lounge, losing time on palace tittle-tattle, and I watch as the schoolgirls settle down on the steps of the pavilion, nestling into its cool pillars, chatting .

The Indian teenagers are ablaze with colour and their traditional dresses worn with narrow trousers are a mixture of eclectic patterned fabrics, dotted with sparkling flecks and trims. As the girls slide between each other they become a kaleidoscope of colour, dappling the courtyard with sparks of sequinned refraction.

I like sequins too. They are a simple design to create shine made by punching small sewable discs from metallic foil or plastic. Easily applied, they can be attached to a style to add instant sparkle, and in a bright light they become resplendent. Sequins are classless, timeless, have a multi-cultural appeal and are an indispensable ingredient in creating glamorous fabrics.

My Indian customers are not far from my mind and I wonder about their motivation for choosing to shop away from home. The wedding will undoubtedly be a lavish affair and, as with many large Indian weddings, there will be numerous events, parties and dress changes. Traditional Indian beadwork is unique, but there may have been a desire to throw a little diversity into their luxurious wedding ward-robes. While sequins are a common denominator of the sparkly dress, shimmering the world over, each culture, each designer has a unique way of crafting embellishment, continually redefining their style and adding novelty to their collections. My designs may lack the intricate metallic thread-work and the spectacle of Indian fashion, but the styles selected are light, feminine and contemporary and may add a little European sassiness into the mix.

The schoolgirls appear to be moving towards me. In a few moments they crowd around me, peering into my sketchbook and giggling at my poor imitations of their youthful styling. They want selfies with me and I stand up to oblige – my interest in cultural dressing is mutual.

In the British Museum a few months previously, I had stopped to study a torn and fraying fragment of early tribal beadwork, musing at the tiny shells and seeds roughly held to the fabric with coarse threads. The design was attractive, and I had considered how easily I could replicate the simple but appealing artwork by replacing the shells with crystal droplets and the seeds with metallic studs. The history of embroidery is fascinating but frustratingly threadbare. Cloth rots, and the earliest examples of embroidery have long since perished. It is well known that Egyptians made glass beads and that embroidered collars were found in Tutankhamun's tomb. So it is easy to imagine that embellishment may date back to the manufacturing of the base cloth itself or when the first eyed needles appeared 40,000 years ago. As I research, I discover that the first found beads date back to 100,000 years BC, so my hunch is that even earlier than that, shortly after caveman style began and the first collection of Palaeolithic rawhide was presented there must have been an inevitable desire to personalise – and what better way to achieve that 'one-of-a-kind' primitive look than to decorate your own clothing?

Some moments of realisation are almost too embarrassing to admit. As I scan my own memories of surface design memorabilia, whizzing between remembered museum treasures and vintage finds, and sweeping through the bookshelves in my studio, tumbling into their pages and extracting imprinted examples of beautiful beadwork, I marvel at my own naivety as the historical importance of tunnelling a hole through a seed finally sinks in.

Embellishment has often become the external manifestation of the human ego. Within the twisted threads of goldwork garnishing ancient ecclesiastical vestments and the pearl-encrusted bodices of Venetian paramours lurks a desire for power. We yearn for recognition, as individuals or as groups, and surface decoration has aided the swift division between those wishing to lead and those ready to be led while establishing unity between the like-minded. Humans compete and impress in order to propel or maintain their position, and embellishment can be a tool to bedazzle others for our own gain. The quality of the workmanship and preciousness of the textures communicates our status and intent and so we trust in each other's ability to decipher our code of dress. While embellishment is not exclusively worn on important occasions, it is at these times that it shines the brightest, reflecting the desire to be acknowledged, desired and respected.

If only I had known this when I was younger. It would have made a convincing argument as I fought with my parents about my wish to skip A levels and begin a foundation course in fashion at the local art college. Surely they would have worried less if I had explained my intention to join the great fraternity of embroiderers – the power-broking experts who stitch with gold to create kings and design splendorous adornment to be worn in the afterlife. But maybe I am getting carried away.

A few days later I am back in Mumbai, standing outside the high-rise household of my new customers, clutching their delivery of dresses. During my trip I have been told they are the richest family in India and that the wedding will be the most expensive in history – but surely, I joke to myself, it will be nothing without *my* gowns. The towering family home has 27 floors, 600 staff and is rumoured to have cost 2.2 billion dollars to build. My aim was to fit the styles in person so I could sneak a peek into this modern-day palace, but they are not at home. Disappointed, I drop the dresses at reception, hope for the best and catch the next plane home.

I have often thought that travel is merely an exploration of pinpricks in the vast surface of things. So I like to revisit the spots I love, getting to know the indentations a place can make on my soul. I adapt quickly to my surroundings and am culturally empathic, so after a few days my London habits fall away and I question the idiosyncrasies of my daily routine. In hotel rooms my collection of portable well-being supplements is ignored and my interest in gluten-free crackers wanes, as does my need to hound my daughters with a daily dose of unwanted advice. I begin to contemplate living in my new place – perhaps for a year. I daydream this existence and relish creating wardrobes for myself, collecting ideas from the stylish inhabitants of my new environment and then I start to fine-tune the outfits in order to decipher the other woman I could be if I didn't go home. How would my appearance change in my new location and how would the shifts in my personal culture manifest themselves; what would I retain of my old self and of my old wardrobe?

In India I would wear colour. Tentatively, I would begin by choosing an ikat woven scarf with subtle hues of navy and green and throw it over my shoulder. Then, a pair of wide-legged pants, sandals in tan leather and market finds of jade and amber bracelets, entwined with mahogany beads wound around my wrists. My Comme des Garçons black shirts and skirts would hang discarded in my wardrobe like Victorian relics as my lust for Keralan vibrancy, boho expat styling, takes off. On an ashram trip I might take in the art of spiritual dressing and make a move towards white linen, and I may even be tempted by a bindi. And then there is pause in my transformation and I pull away from the *Eat Pray Love* look and yearn for some familiar structure – perhaps shoulder pads and socks. The true evolution of Jaipur Jenny can now begin to take form. Selecting a Nehru-collared kurta – indigo with black printed paisleys – and drawstring pyjamas combined with an androgynous suit jacket, a pair of Nike trainers, I could attempt to cross the divide between India's traditional richness and its westward-facing materialism.

In the South of France, I would rent a house and stay until my paleness warmed to a golden tan, cultivating a taste for pastis. Only then would I dare to wear the ubiquitous embroidered dresses in white, my nemesis shade, and cycle into town to collect metallic leather flip-flops and ivory cotton espadrilles, straw hats and stacking rings. This would keep me busy for a while but, even as I write this, I am bothered by the idea of Provençal beige linen homeware and the scent of lavender oil. I am worried about my compatibility with these new surroundings and I accept that this particular wardrobe fantasy is perhaps a step too far for me. I would be a fraudulent fashion follower, as I seem to do 'summer casual' with reluctance and am out of my depth when it comes to beachwear style.

Perhaps my style is better suited to cities, where smartness is preferred and anonymity provides a flexibility in effort. I suspect I am a rather like Kate Adie, the BBC correspondent who famously combined her flak jacket with a pair of pearl earrings when she reported from the frontline of the Gulf war. While she was mocked for her accessorising, I imagine she may have felt some comfort in keeping a sense of her identity on show, and I think a subtler shift would be better for me, too, so I could blend my most treasured items with sympathetic finds from my new homeland in order to retain a semblance of Englishness.

Changing how we dress can mean we are perceived differently. Subconsciously we scan each other looking for clues as to the potential viability of a new relationship, or to gauge the emotional state of a friend. We dress to impress, to further our ambitions to win money, power and love.

While books on self-improvement offer us suggestions to evolve through language and mindfulness, perhaps with our choice of clothing we still – unwittingly – give ourselves up to the world around. As I survey the bookshop shelves, crammed with pages of advice to help us navigate the complexity of our new era, I see that the common theme is to change ourselves. The hard-fought battle to shift our habits, ingrained through cultural and familial coding, threatens our uniqueness and the ways in which we have naturally evolved to navigate our course. My playful dalliance with cultural appropriation on my travels triggers thoughts on how clothing is maligned in the essays on directed self-evolution.

It is often suggested that, in order to trigger change, a good place to start is by pretending. Perhaps as I write I am merely pretending to be a writer, but by finishing this book I will be a writer. I imagine what I will wear when I am interviewed by the press about this book. Maybe I will fall into the world of English scribes, taking style tips from Daphne du Maurier or Zadie Smith to create a bohemian vibe that prods an audience into accepting me as such. In the contemporary world, artists can no longer afford to hide behind their work. Recognised geniuses may be able to evade the act of self-portrayal required to promote one's work. But most of us need to embellish.

WHITE

The Victoria and Albert Museum archives are stored in Blythe House, an imposing Edwardian building tucked away behind the Olympia Exhibition Centre in West Kensington. I am visiting the Clothworkers' Centre, the fashion and textiles department of the museum, to view some wedding gowns.

The wide, square table in front of me is covered in white tissue and the first of the gowns is laid out, covering almost its entire surface. I have instructions not to touch the fabric, and if I wish the garment to be moved, to look inside, I must make a request at the desk. I have been given a stainless steel trolley on which to put my equipment and I have placed my sketchbook and pencil at the ready. It has taken a while to get to this point – application forms, registration on arrival, security checks – and now my belongings have been taken away and put in a locker. I have been given a two-hour slot and am eager to start.

To spend time alone with such beautiful garments is a privilege. The thrill begins with the colour and fabric, the design and provenance. And then, fascinated by the construction and detailing, I look closer to see the grubby, knotted threads, fraying seams and sweat-stained underarms and suddenly I am unravelling time, as humanity and history collide.

The ceiling here is high, with spotlights positioned on a dropped metal frame, and the walls are covered with cold, creamy enamel-coated brickwork. The windows are obscured by gauzy blinds blocking out the spring skies and the room is deathly quiet. There are six tables set out in a grid and on each one is laid a body-sized topping of crumpled fabric. Today, these vintage gowns appear to me like shed skin.

For a moment I feel like a Nordic noir detective visiting the pathology department to get an autopsy report. As I glance around the room, this weird thought gives me a profound insight into my motivation for designing bridalwear. It's the preciousness of it all. To create something that will linger, collecting dust and interest, for decades – perhaps even centuries – fuels my passion for making memorable clothing and, as I stand among these offcuts of exceptional moments, this feeling has never been more pertinent. To dare to dream that my own designs may someday be coveted in this way and treated with such reverence gives my work purpose.

I move to the side of the table and climb a stepladder so that I can photograph the items from above. Below me is a two-piece Victorian bridal ensemble. There is an ornately embroidered, satin duchess skirt and beside it a small riding-style jacket buttoned with large pearls. The narrow sleeves and bodice have been stuffed with rolled tissue, both to give form to the bodice and to protect the fabric. The colour is a delicate shade of ivory and the satin softly undulates, casting shadows on itself. I circle the garments. The detail is exquisite. The skirt is made up of tulle and silk panels that are about 15cm wide and run down the skirt from top to bottom, embellished with a hand-embroidered leaf design topped with a generous scattering of beadwork. Sprouting from each tendril is a lily of the valley, seed pearls peeping from beneath the petals, and I wonder whether the bride, like myself, had a particular fondness for this flower.

I want to spend more time with this piece, but I am also impatient to see the other dresses in the room. I take a quick tour.

On the next table is Elizabeth Emanuel's wedding gown, designed by Zandra Rhodes. As I study the dress, I wonder why Emanuel decided against designing her own. Perhaps, like me, she was in awe of Rhodes' hand-printed and cleverly cut whimsical wonders. It is a classic chiffon style from the designer, decorated with swirls of wandering tendrils, delicate fluted sleeves and a gently gathered skirt. The gown looks like a wilted version of itself now and quite the opposite of the image I have of the Emanuels' crowning achievement: Princess Diana's wedding dress. Remembering it, I take a moment to drift back to 1981.

The Royal Wedding was a Big Day, and as 700 million around the world crowded around their televisions waiting for a glimpse of the bride I was upstairs in my bedroom making a birthday card for an unrequited love. I remember my annoyance at being interrupted by my mother and forced to come downstairs to watch one of the most important fashion moments in history. But as I sat on the sofa with my arms folded tightly across my chest, biting my lip and fighting hopelessly against pubescent rage, my heart secretly melted. As Diana stepped out from her carriage onto the steps of St Paul's Cathedral, the world's oxygen levels must have dropped as we all gasped. However, a taffetorial disaster appeared to be taking place: the beautiful young princess seemed to be surrounded by crumpled fabric. The young designers moved quickly to rescue their design and skilfully tamed the metres of unruly silk, stepping back to reveal one of the most magical dresses in bridal history. I broke out of my teenage strop and smiled. On reflection, that afternoon was a seminal moment for both Diana and myself. As she left St Paul's a princess, I returned to my bedroom and I began to sketch my first bridal dress.

The other dresses I had chosen to view that day at the V&A archives, including a Balmain ballgown and an unusual 1930s dress that seemed more Jane Austen than Greta Garbo, didn't hold my attention for long and, after taking photographs of them, I returned to my Victorian bride. I wanted to get to know her.

The forensics begin. She is petite, with a tiny waist of about 22 inches, slight shoulders and, at a guess, she is 5 feet 2 inches tall. Her frame seems childlike, but I know from my years of rifling through vintage clothing that people were simply smaller in those days and the average age of a bride in the late 1800s was 22. My bride may be slim but she was not lacking. The dress has wealth woven all over it, from the sumptuousness of the silk to the accordion-pleated trim around the sweeping hem of the skirt. I look closer. Around the edge of the basque-style jacket are two layers of carefully sewn piping. Many dresses of this era had a floral garland trailing around their borders, and I imagine that this beautiful detail may have been lost.

Piping around such sharp corners is difficult to do without creating bulk, so it must have been sewn by an expert hand. More than likely the dress was a couture creation.

I ask to see the inside of the jacket and, with white-gloved hands, a young woman from the museum's team carefully unbuttons the bodice for me – almost in slow motion. As I peep inside I feel a rush of excitement. These are the 'workings' of the garment, and for a moment I can hear distant voices exchanging views on where to best align the stays to support the desired shape, and whether they should be steel or featherbone, to give more flexibility. The jacket's seams are neatly snipped to allow for the undulating waist and shapely bust, and perhaps the seam-stresses would have conferred on the finishing of the seams before deciding to whip the edges with cotton thread. I could so easily slip into these conversations; those we have in my own studio are not so different. The language of dressmakers seems to transcend centuries and cultures.

I decide to sketch, so I sit on a stool to study the cuff of the jacket's little sleeve. As I start to draw the eclectic combination of folded satin, ruffled tulle and delicate fringing, an overwhelming desire to know this woman takes hold of me. My impatience grows as I doodle the fringe of stained faux pearls and I realise I am no longer concentrating. I put down my pencil and go to ask if there is any information on this particular dress and bride.

The young woman behind the desk informs me that they have very few details of the owners of these designs, but are much more likely to have some information relating to their designers. I cross my fingers and wait.

She returns with two names for me – both bride and designer. The former's name was Clara Mathews, who was aged 25 when she married Colonel Hugh Stafford (who was 46) at St George's Church, Hanover Square, on 19 February 1880. I am not surprised to learn that the dress was designed by Charles Worth. A British designer, Worth is credited with founding the French couture industry when, in 1858, he opened the doors to his own atelier in Paris. Worth was a great innovator, and his talents for self-publicising, combined with his exquisite sense of style and revolutionary business ideas, turned the world of fashion upside down. The prices of bespoke gowns soared and clients were invited for a private consultation with the designer at the atelier, reversing the traditional relationships between customer and dressmaker. Worth stitched his name into the garments and labelled luxury began.

Despite its decadent embellishment, the dress he made for Clara has understated elegance and is made to perfection. The three-piece wedding gown with a separate train was the favoured look of this time, and Clara's high-necked jacket is a statement piece of tailored sophistication that makes this design both remarkable and very Worth.

The information I received that morning was limited, but the most startling snippet was that Clara was the daughter of Isaac Merritt Singer, the great pioneer of the sewing machine. I had always assumed that Singer was the inventor but, after a little research, I find that although the prototype was not actually his work, he was the genius behind its design development and commercial distribution. I also discover that Clara was illegitimate. Born in New York in 1855, she was forced to flee the US with her mother, Mary, and Singer following his arrest for bigamy. An actor and businessman, Singer had fathered 24 children by the time of his death in 1875.

It crosses my mind that 'Singer' was probably one of the first words I encountered as a child. Sitting on the floor of my grandmother's house, I would watch the coal fire flames jumping and listen to the mechanical whirl of her Hand Crank Singer, the ornate golden logo gleaming against the machine's dark body. My grandmother Gertrude Smith was a dressmaker and the furniture in her small house was decorated with haphazard piles of folded floral textiles, the carpet thick with embedded cotton threads and the occasional pin. Her machine is now resting on a shelf in my office, a shrine to a woman who could cut clever corners on rationed meterage to keep a community in the latest looks.

It has been said that sewing can mend your soul and, if that is the case, Singer can be forgiven for his wayward ways in return for saving so many. The commercial sewing machine brought creativity and employment into the home at an affordable price, seamlessly propelling fashion forward at the rate of 900 stitches a minute.

For Clara, 1880 was a good time to wed. The Married Women's Property Act of 1874 gave wealthy brides the right to control their own earnings and assets. This was quite a moment in bridal history and for women. Liberated from the constraints of a marriage contract, women must have felt an exciting new sense of empowerment. This was reflected in the aesthetics of the ceremony, with the well-heeled and stylish breaking free from what was traditionally a small and private event, choosing instead to go public with large and lavish church weddings with all the trimmings.

I have now turned from pathologist to fashion sleuth and, later that week, finding myself between appointments in Mayfair, I walk west towards St George's Church, where Clara was married. From Hanover Square I can see the grey stone church towering above the pavement, its large

Corinthian columns leaning into the busy street. For a parish church, it is quite imposing.

Inside, I sit at one of the pews towards the back, on the aisle side. Despite its bright stained-glass windows and the vaulted ceiling trimmed with gold edged mouldings, the church is drowning in dark panelling and Gothic detail. I try to decipher the original décor, picturing the interior swathed in bouquets of sweet-scented myrtles. Meanwhile, an elderly man is vacuuming between the pews on the groom's side and the organist has gone rogue, so I close my eyes in an effort to escape the cacophony. A noise from the street startles me and I turn to look towards the entrance, and it is then that I see her: Clara. Her face is framed by a blaze of auburn ringlets, and a corsage of trailing scented blossom scoops the curls from her neck, revealing the softly gathered lace trim around her collar. The fabric of her skirt and jacket is illuminated by the light, starched and brighter than I remember. I can almost hear the pearly fringing gently tapping against itself, creating a soft rattle, and the rustle of her skirt, the heavy layers of cotton and silk colliding and folding as she steps towards me into the church. She lifts her gaze and I recognise her look of shy excitement – and then she is gone.

Clara, I discover, had five children and lost two of them in infancy in a marriage that lasted only 13 years (Hugh died in 1893). Sadly, I have been unable to find a photograph of Clara and Hugh's wedding day, so I admit my apparition is fantastical. But it is because of her dress that I know she lived at all, and now, more than a century later, it is this garment that has opened a portal into the past for me to explore.

There are few articles of clothing that define moments, let alone a life; over centuries of female marginalisation, perhaps the wedding dress has been so coveted for reasons other than just the desire to document a day. History seems to lie between the threads, tricking us with sentimentality, encouraging us to hold on to these lacy remnants – and in doing so both the forgotten bride and woman are remembered. The historical gown can be indicative of the fine line between youthfulness and maturity, the veiled entry into married life, catching the moment of transition and encapsulating the before and after.

The wedding dress is, indeed, a garment suffused with emotion. It begins to take form in childhood daydreams and later becomes the souvenir of an unforgettable day, a symbol of hope and victorious love. And from this, I dare to steal a little creative immortality for myself. Neatly folded in tissue, my dresses will be stored away, gently becoming old-fashioned with the passing of time. Perhaps one of my designs will adorn an archive table, a romantic imprint to be studied, sketched and handled with care while awaiting reincarnation. After all, for a designer, surely the highest compliment you can receive is to be invited to become part of this very special day and, perhaps, part of history too.

'Wow! I look so beautiful!' the young woman exclaimed.

She stood in front of a large mirror, mesmerised by her own appearance. The room of chatting women fell silent, stunned by this anomalous statement. We were presenting a new bridal collection and our shop in Belgravia was teeming with brides-to-be and their mothers and friends. This particular woman was wearing a full-skirted bridal gown that was two sizes too small and gaping open at the back. Her hair was tousled onto the top of her head, and she was about to cry. However, it was not her appearance that held everyone transfixed, it was the surprising moment of self-appreciation. It's rare, unfortunately, to hear women talking about how great they look. For me, her candidness encapsulated the rules of designing a good wedding dress. In brief: I must create a beautiful gown, a bride must fall in love with it and then she should be overwhelmed by how she looks and feels – sometimes so overwhelmed that tears follow.

I have stood before many brides as they try on their dresses, and as they look past me into their reflection I have been enthralled and fascinated by what appears to be an innate sense of joy. Occasionally, I have lifted a veil over a bride's face and been taken aback by her sudden outpouring of emotion. As the tears give way to laughter, I am reminded that before the veil became a romantic haze for the contemporary bride, it helped to hide the despair of a heavy-hearted wife-to-be, coerced into an unhappy coupling.

To design a bridal collection of about 30 pieces, I need a story, a romantic scenario to capture the heart of a bride. *A Midsummer Night's Dream*, the beguiling Shakespeare comedy set in an enchanted forest, for example, offers endless inspiration for celestial opulence and otherworldly detail. Titania, queen of the fairies, is the perfect muse. Meanwhile, the decadence of F. Scott Fitzgerald's novel *The Great Gatsby*, a portrait of the Roaring Twenties and the obsessional love story between a millionaire and a debutante, is a recurring theme in my past collections. Gatsby's wild parties, devised to attract the attention of his unsuspecting love Daisy, reflect an era en route to self-destruction, the last sparks of hedonism burning brightly. The deco influence, the seductive dance between the protagonists and the striking fashion styling of the time are a go-to for inspiration.

I have also explored the lens-based work of Madame Yevonde. At the dawn of colour photography, Yevonde captured society women as mythological heroines dressed in classical costumes from the ancient world. The collection of photographic portraits entitled 'The Goddesses' included Ariadne, Persephone and Venus. These stylised images printed in soft pastel hues are hauntingly beautiful tributes to the contemporary women of the 1930s. My collection that season was ethereal and diaphanous, mirroring the mythical narrative of feminine virtue.

The contemporary wedding is in itself an inspiring resource. On Pinterest I find dreamy images of candlelit tables winding through forest enclaves and nuptials on white sandy beaches. The desire to express individuality, coupled with a wanderlust imagination, has encouraged Instagrammable epics of wedding day self-expression. Social media has supercharged bridal design, awakening designers to a brave new world. Almost overnight, necklines plummeted and hip-cinching skirts revealed the contours of a generation of selfie-loving young women. Trends have shifted away from historical influences to the allure of Hollywood, with the 'red-carpet moment' becoming the aspirational ideal and the word 'sexy' echoing through the bridal boutiques of the land, shaking the rails of conventionality.

I recently visited the Fashion Museum in Bath to meet the museum's curator Rosemary Harden. While exploring the museum's archive of nineteenth-century styles, we discussed the evolution of bridal trends. Rosemary informed me that, historically, it has been royal brides who have nudged styles in a new direction. When the young Queen Victoria married Albert in 1840, her dress of white satin and Honiton lace, trimmed with garlands of orange blossom, caused a step change in bridal history. While wearing white was not an unusual choice for the time, her endorsement caught the imagination of generations to come. It is fascinating that throughout recent history's political upheavals, the emancipation of women and the social media revolution, wearing white has been a relentless phenomenon.

As I look through early wedding photography, I wonder whether it was by chance that wearing white coincided with the invention of the daguerreotype, the first commercially viable photography process. Victoria and Albert were one of the first couples to have their wedding day immortalised in this way. It was fashionable at this time for brides to wear a favourite-coloured dress or to invest in a new formal style that could be worn again at important occasions. But, given that even the brightest of scarlet gowns or prettiest florals would become muddy tones of grey in print, it wasn't long before brides realised that wearing white illuminated their presence and pulled into focus their sartorial beauty.

White has symbolic resonance too and has been used to portray innocence – the unsullied heart and sexual purity of the bride. It is also a tough colour to keep clean. To create white cloth, fabric must be heavily processed, and the inevitable wastage due to natural imperfections is costly. But like many fashion trends, the most challenging option often becomes the most desired. So, in the past, wearing white suggested status and wealth, as only the rich and powerful could afford to keep such garments spotless.

It is also an ethereal colour, the garb of ghosts and angels, and while the white wedding dress has become a symbol of romantic love the world over, its spiritual significance still lingers. The wearing of white is synonymous with the entry into an alternative state, the certified moments of life – birth, marriage and death. It is at these times we seem to desire a separation from everyday fashions, perhaps finding comfort in tradition and turning to otherworldliness to emphasise the profundity of the occasion. When Queen Victoria was buried her bridal veil was placed over her face, an emblematic declaration of her love even in death.

My own wedding dress was dove grey and the most challenging dress I have ever designed. I am altruistic when I sketch and, unlike many designers whose work revolves around their personal style, I am never my own muse.

Putting myself in the position of the client sent me into a spin, so rather than fantasising about the end product, I concentrated on the process, choosing the fabric, the colour and the construction of the garment.

I chose dove grey because it was as far as I could bring myself to stray from my wardrobe of mostly black; besides, after 28 years with my partner I wasn't about to play the role of a virgin goddess.

However, like most brides I wanted extravagance, the once-in-a-lifetime gown. After seasons of selecting fabrics within a certain budget, I chose an expensive Austrian guipure lace and created a 'seamless' dress by interlocking the lace to mould around my body, stitched by hand, couture style. It was a simple shape, midi length with a high neck and small shoulder pads to balance my pear-shaped figure. I scattered the lace with Swarovski crystals and Christian Louboutin made me some matching heels. My dress made me feel elegant and was also true to my understated style, while the invisible seams were a designer's guilty pleasure. I also chose to wear a headband with a small mesh veil dappled with tiny rhinestones, which hugged my face, masking my eyes. I am an introvert by nature, just stepping out occasionally to support my passions, and I found this flimsy barrier of sparkly tulle gave me a little buffer from so much attention.

As with many brides, my dress remained a mystery to my partner until the day of our wedding. The 'unseen' dress is now part of the romantic foreplay of wedding preparations, as is the 'reveal', when the groom turns to face his wife-to-be and smiles. However, like many bridal traditions this custom has dark roots. When contractual marriages were customary, the bride was encouraged to arrive just moments before signing her estate away in case the groom felt tempted to turn on his heel and run. This custom has survived generations, gently transforming itself from a moment of trepidation to one of excitement, from devious ensnarement to romantic union.

As I design a bridal collection, each dress must have its own divine inspiration – to create both the drama and excitement the bride desires – and often the origins of these ideas are quite diverse. In the back row of a classical music concert in Mallorca, I was struggling to stay awake so I doodled a lace-backed gown with a draped chiffon bodice and copied the sleeve detail from the blouse of a woman three rows in front. The gown that followed is named 'Aspen' and has a deep V bodice and a sweeping chiffon skirt that gently fish-tails from the hip, flowing into a dramatic train. The advertising image for this dress, shot in the doorway of a Malibu villa, the Pacific Ocean glimmering in the background, created a wave of interest and it quickly became a bestseller. Later, in 2012, the Duchess of Cambridge wore an emerald version of the gown to the London Olympic Gala Reception at the Royal Albert Hall.

Another time, during Paris Fashion Week in 2005, I found myself with a few hours to spare and visited the Musée des Arts Décoratifs. Its permanent collection of jewels is a sparkling cave of spotlit treats celebrating the artistry of jewellery through the ages, and it is one of my favourite haunts. Exhibits of unearthed clay pots, sharpened flints and shrivelled bodies often fail to connect me to ancient civilisations, but show me a museum case of beaten gold rings with crudely set gems, strings of turquoise beads and cleverly carved whalebone hair-combs and suddenly the uncut thread of woman's relentless desire for adornment pulls taut. I know the fondness felt for these possessions and the centuries fall away as I find synergy with these women through their jewels.

In the museum that day I found an inspirational piece of the sort that can instantly give life to a dress – the 'Sylvia' pendant designed by Paul and Henri Vever in 1900. All I needed to do was superimpose the detail onto the silhouette of a dress. It is a strange but exquisite piece of jewellery, half woman, half butterfly. The insect-like anatomy is forged with jade enamelling and diamond studs, creating winged opulence. This detailing is artfully shaped into an Edwardian dress and mounted on to an alabaster female form, with large red rubies clasped within a sparkling bodice and a skirt of golden drapery. I gratefully absorbed this art nouveau treasure and stole its delicate patterning and symmetry. The dress it inspired – the 'Papillon' gown – is ethereal and romantic, its fluid layers of tulle falling from under the bust to form crystal-edged wings with delicate veins of cut-glass beads, the bodice embedded with would-be diamonds.

'Something old, something new, something borrowed, something blue' is a line from a late-nineteenth-century poem, later adopted as a must-have list of lucky items for a bride's glory box. Nowadays, the dress is generally considered the 'new' component and many brides will hunt for a style that will escape the judgement of time. Only with hindsight will the puff of a sleeve or the voluptuousness of a bow show themselves as moments of madness. But, as I flip through my glossy books of legendary gowns, some of my personal favourites are the wedding dresses worn by those who chose to live in the moment, taking a fashion trend to new extremes, the daredevils, the crusaders for change – or those who consider their marriage only the first of many! Despite my adherence to designing commercial trends, I am rebellious in my scrapbooking of bridal fashion. The amalgamation of my red- and white-carpet dressing nestles my preferences somewhere in between and I secretly long to design for an irreverent bride.

Nevertheless, there are some undisputed classics. The image of Bianca Jagger in her crisp white trouser suit, sheltering under the Riviera sky in her wide-brimmed hat, is legendary. Her androgynous spin on seventies suiting established Jagger as the ultimate glam rock bride and an aspirational icon in chic registry office dressing. In 1969, Audrey Hepburn (at her second wedding) once again wore Givenchy. The dress, a pale pink mini with matching headscarf, playfully personified the social movement of the time by mimicking the everyday dress of a sixties housewife. However, when Carolyn Bessette married Robert Kennedy Jr in a Narciso Rodriguez slip, she became the cat that got the cream. The simplicity of her satin sheath, effortless and understated, was a glitch in the history of bridal fashions and its ironic timelessness still prevails.

To be swayed by history is inevitable, but to create something contemporary is the aim; likewise, we are attracted to what we know but also tempted by the unexpected. To scatter crystallised snowflakes onto a winter wedding cape or to slash the neckline of a dress low enough to raise eyebrows is often as daring as required. Few brides want to risk ridicule, and therefore silhouettes shift slowly. But with the growth of same-sex marriages, transgender brides and millennial confidence, perhaps I can look forward to designing for a more egalitarian generation who will blow away the cobwebs from bridal fashion. Or perhaps the current political instability and economic uncertainty may boomerang trends into retro comfort and, while liberation has in recent years given way to a lightness of touch, the cushioning of a petticoated crinoline and the support of a structured bodice may offer some solace against the realities of the world we wed in.

SHOW

'I want the shoes to be ... cunty,' said Pat.

I have a way of dislocating myself from uncomfortable situations. Teleporting myself to the other side of the room so that I am not fully present, I watch the scene unfold – half in, half out. But sometimes I just want a different perspective, and I had the feeling I would want to remember this particular encounter from every angle. So, as I took a deep breath and nodded in agreement, 'Yes cunty, yes that would be good,' I began to immerse myself – from a distance.

Patricia Field's Lower East Side Manhattan home was reminiscent of a Studio 54 VIP hang-out. Of course, I am only speculating; Schrager, the club's impresario, had been to prison by the time I could order a drink – but I've seen the photos and get the vibe. The spacious apartment was strewn with fake leopardskin and tubular chrome furniture, wall-to-wall mirrors, a bar – and more than a dash of hot pink. It was cool in a sexy, kitsch kind of way and I was excited to be there. Pat, the legendary redhead, the wardrobe mistress and design guru behind *Sex and the City*, had agreed to be our show stylist for the season and we were sat on the floor of her apartment, surrounded by my design sketches and fabric swatches, eager to get Pat's take on things. Pat took my sketchbook and began to illustrate a 'cunty shoe' while her dog, a toy something or other, began to rut her foot, vigorously. Pat obliged the dog by wiggling her toes and continued to draw a rather impractical stiletto, reversing over her lines as she began to elaborate on the inspiration behind 'cunty'.

I hate that word; it makes me jump. Germaine Greer, who attempted to liberalise it in the seventies, to make it ordinary and take away its malice, recently reflected on her perverse pleasure at her failure to do so. The word has maintained its power to shock and is considered by most to be the utterance of last resort. So, to be honest, I was struggling with Pat's unexpected use of the word – but at the same time, I was curious.

The collection had begun to take shape during a family holiday in Egypt with our two young daughters. In Cairo, as they ran through the tombs in the Valley of the Kings, I had memorised the patterns on the walls and en route to 'see dead people' in the Egyptian Museum, the must-see mummies, I had stopped to sketch the patterns sweeping around a pharaoh's chariot. The holiday had given me a rich bounty for a collection of decorative indulgence, but, was its inspiration just a little too obvious? Luckily, Pat was about to fix that by insisting we style the models as beautiful young women tumbling out of a nightclub in the early hours of the morning, a little worse for wear, walking the streets in the afterglow of a raucous night out.

This is where the synthesis between designer and stylist begins. At the point when I am able to show sketches, my own concept of the collection is often well formed and, while the initial meeting is something I relish, I am often challenged by the stylist's fresh perspective. Ultimately, however, that's the aim – to toss me out of my comfort zone. A good stylist will nudge a designer forward by suggesting ways to create excitement around a collection to satisfy the appetite of the fashion press while maintaining the brand's integrity. My aim is to create styles to sell and to keep my business alive, and I need to balance the stylist's creativity with my customers' requirements. So we work together to spark up the must-have gowns and experiment with new silhouettes. On occasion, the more radical the stylist's take on a particular collection, the more successful the collaboration has become, elevating the brand to a new level of interest. Timeless classics may sell but they don't necessarily inspire the front row. So, to partner with a strong stylist, someone with their finger on the pulse and the skill to give an unexpected edge to my work, is often worth the reimbursement they demand.

Our first stylist, Claudia Navone, took my second show collection of sixties-inspired looks full spin by matching my skater-skirted styles with pastel-feathered bonnets boasting dangling oversized pompoms. Claudia, the epitome of Italian elegance, chose low-heeled, metallic T-bars by Emma Hope and brushed the models' hair into slick high-top chignons. And, when Grace Cobb, the then fashion director of *The Face*, joined us for our spring/summer 2004 collection, she pushed our St Tropez-inspired collection of hedonistic poolside glamour – high-cut swimsuits and silky throw-ons – into the deep end by styling up Lizzy Jagger in sky-scraper silver platforms, a mop of Marie Helvin-esque curls and a gooey pout of sunset orange. Later, as rumour has it, Courtney Love was removed from a flight wearing Lizzy's lime-coloured, low-cut baby-doll style – the one she wore in the show – and I enjoyed a pang of pleasure at Love's sybaritic indulgence; it seemed to fit the mood of the collection.

Pat flew to London when the collection was nearly complete and we spent the day in my studio styling up the looks ready for our catwalk show in Milan. It wasn't an easy day. I physically flinched when, on returning to my office, I found the model posed with a pair of white fishnet tights, cut into a wide band and pulled over her face, her nose poking through a hole. And later, the thrill of being in the presence of three of my living fashion icons – Pat, make-up queen Charlotte Tilbury and hair stylist Sam McKnight – was crushed when Pat caused a scene by overriding their contributions, demanding a whole new level of 'pulled through a hedge backwards' hair and 'druggy eyes'. The team dealt with Pat's outburst as professionally as possible, but once we got to Milan, Pat having been unable to make it, we guiltily smoothed out the models' hair into a more glamorous mess.

However, her genius was her strength of vision and gutsy willingness to experiment. Her inspiration was succinct and everyone involved 'got it'. That season we worked with Siobhan Fahey (of Bananarama) to create the soundtrack for the show and, in her house in north London, as I relayed Pat's anti-glam mantra, the 'cunty' heels and tornado-swept hair, Siobhan and her partner just nodded, loving the kickass inspiration. It was music to their ears and they quickly put together some aptly grungy tracks, setting the scene for the catwalk.

Now, as I scan the images of the collection, I recognise the Egyptian influences; scarab-beetle-blue sequins shimmer on the gowns and the minidresses with golden borders of swirling thread-work take me back to watching my daughters play hide-and-seek around the ancient pillars of Luxor. I am my harshest critic and tend to see past endeavours largely as a reason to try harder next time. It's a cruel characteristic but I have softened towards my early work and am now charmed by its energy and naivety. However, it is Patricia Field's contributions – the necklaces of sink-plug ball-chain (bought from a Kentish Town hardware store), the studded wristbands wrapped over leatherette gloves, and of course the 'cunty' shoes, my favourite ever Louboutins – that make me smile most.

The Debenhams fashion show was the highlight of my seasonal calendar in the early 1970s. My mum and I would arrive early for a vanilla slice in the store's café and then take the lift up to Ladieswear. I would perch on my mum's lap and the show would begin – gingham, polyester, needlecord, seersucker, maxi, mini, raglan and princess line – it was an early learning class for kids with textural inclinations. Then, as I peeked between the shoulders of the front row to catch a glimpse of the models, my mum would whisper in my ear, 'Love that dress – but her face is a bit funny, isn't it?' I would giggle and she would tell me to stop, and when I did stop she would say, 'That would look nice on my kitchen table,' and I'd giggle again. I loved giggling and I loved fashion shows – from the get-go.

But when did *the* fashion show get going? The first designer shows, held in the salons of the Parisian designer houses of Charles Worth and Lucile, were small and intimate events, with the models roaming through resplendent rooms showing the designer's latest collections to a high-society audience of empresses and princesses interspersed with actresses, dancers and singers (the theatrical elite of the time) – the designer's couture clients. However, seasonal private presentations by dressmakers and fabric merchants to entice the wealthy to say yes to a dress had been under way for centuries.

In the early 1900s, fashion's revolutionary designer, Paul Poiret, took his show on the road to attract new clients from Europe's most affluent and influential cities. Poiret's shows were extravagant fusions of art and fashion and he set the stage for fashion shows to become the multi-sensory spectacles they are today.

Unfortunately for Poiret, the extravagance of his catwalks and his lifestyle were too costly and, after the demand for his designs declined, the man believed to have created the first-ever fashion photo shoot, and who finally freed women from the corset, died penniless. (Note to self: the destitute, aging designer is not an uncommon phenomenon. Is there an insurance policy for becoming 'unfashionable'?)

From that time onwards, fashion shows became glamorous occasions not to be missed, and the American department stores quickly took inspiration from couturiers, imitating both the salon-style format and their designs to market their own seasonal collections. In the 1960s, when designer ready-to-wear took to the catwalks for the first time, presenting accessible fashion in a more energetic and experimental style, women's interest in the latest hem lengths hit new highs. These shows were exclusive events for store buyers, VIPs and the fashion press, and initially photographers were not permitted, just in case a newly shaped sleeve or shifted waistline found its way into the mind of a rival creator, plus to ensure the designs were kept snugly under wraps until they were unveiled, in store, months later. However, women's patience has since waned from the six-monthly seasonal reveal to a mere nanosecond and designers' catwalk collections are now live-streamed worldwide.

The passion to create is so often closely followed by the compulsion to show our efforts to others – to receive validation and to capture the imagination of your audience so that there will be a means to continue, to evolve and repeat.

The emotive nature of fashion provides a designer with endless ways to present their collections to gain press support and to trigger consumer interest. But is that it? A show is a means to build a brand and to sell a product, but for a designer the experience also nourishes the creative ego – the addiction to creating something relevant, eye-catching, beautiful and inspirational.

In my first term at St Martins, I discovered the exciting allure of the 'show' and perhaps it was this experience that triggered an ambition to have my own show one day. It was Fashion Week and the class was despatched to see the catwalks – armed with a schedule and instructions to 'dress up, push in, and get in!' I was always happy to 'dress up', but 'pushing in' and hustling my way past the scary monsters of London's 1984 fashion hierarchy was a daunting prospect.

At dusk outside Kensington Olympia a crowd was gathering, jostling their way towards the entrance, the epicentre of a very stylish scrum. For a moment I stood in a clearing, looking on, devising a strategy. This situation would take more than just a nudge from a Sue Ellen shoulder pad or a winklepickered kick. Should I try to power-dress my way through, waving at an imaginary friend, or make myself small and invisible, camouflaged by the crowd, who like myself were all dressed in black? My new college friends had dispersed shortly after we had arrived, having mutually acknowledged that this was to be an each-to-their-own endeavour; to be viewed as nothing more than a bunch of fashion students would undoubtedly hinder our chances of success. So now, alone, I was ready to make my move. I took a deep breath and dived down beneath the press teams, ducking between raw-edged ruffles by Comme des Garçons while pleated frills of crispy silk taffeta flicked against my ears. As I pushed ahead, I imparted a smudge of Miss Selfridge Copper Knockers lipstick to a pair of leatherette leggings before coming up for air, thrilled to find that I had made it to the other side and into the grandiose Pillar Hall – the setting for the Zandra Rhodes show and my first ever designer catwalk experience.

I quickly found myself a pillar and hid behind it until the lights dimmed, then slid around to watch the show. It was more theatre than fashion, with changing sets and choreo-graphed formations of pin-thin models twirling, floating in unison and posing with hands on hips – the eighties power pose with a killer stare. The intricately printed and embroidered fabrics and lurex weaves caught the spot-lights, and the models became sparkling mirrorballs. I was entranced. I won't pretend I can remember more – but I can recall feeling torn between wanting the show to go on forever and wishing to get back to my little room at the halls of residence as soon as I could and sketch!

How wonderful to hear from you and fabulous that you remember my magnificent Pillar room show in 1984. Was it Spring Summer — my Fables of the Sea collection — or The Magic Carpet — Autumn Winter? X Zandra

Hi Zandra, I am really not sure exactly — but I definitely either floated or flew home!

Not far from London, just off the M1 in a large industrial warehouse, my life's work is stored — an archive of our show collections, zipped up into black cloth dress bags and suspended on metres of hanging rails. It always seems to be grey and raining when I go there, but as soon as we pull into the car park and turn off the windscreen wipers, I feel bright with anticipation: I am about to visit my very own secret treasure trove.

But first I am given a fluorescent orange waistcoat to put on and taken through the health and safety procedures by a young woman, the gatekeeper. She hands me a mug of lukewarm green tea and leads me through a series of interlocking doors and narrow corridors before we arrive in a large, open storeroom. I put my bag down and make my way to the furthest rail. As I begin to unzip the first bag, my new designer, whom I have brought to the archive as part of his induction into the brand, calls out to me from behind a rail.

'You used to be so sexy!' he says, holding up a pair of gold leather hot pants. 'I know, I know,' I murmur, amused by his comment and taking a quick look at my reflection in a partition window. But in an instant my mind flips back to September 2006. Rosie Huntington-Whiteley, fresh faced and probably only 15 years old, is catwalking the length of our studio, barefoot and wearing the hot pants with a white chiffon blouse. It was her first season at London Fashion Week and the buzz around her was gaining momentum. I instantly liked her and remember vividly her Bardot-like magnetism, but it was her palpable eagerness that attracted me – I got the feeling she was bubbling to get going with being a model, so I booked her immediately.

I go back to opening the bag and out the dresses tumble – and with them everything else. My head feels as if it will explode as my memories resurface in a stream of flicking hi-res images, and the glimpse of sparkly-edged tulle and a waistband of tiny crystals glimmering beneath the trans- parent film of the cellophane covers is enough to take me back in time and my life begins to flash before me. The bags are packed too tightly and the dresses are crushed, so I release the cord, holding the hangers by their necks, and spread out the styles. Then I pull away the dress bags and stand back. Rich ruby satins, amethyst and rose quartz tulle – autumn/winter 2004.

It was to be our fourth catwalk show and due to the success of the previous season – the 'Riviera pool party' – we had secured a serious sponsorship package and an impressive guest list. The inspiration? The Ballets Russes. So it wasn't a coincidence that we had chosen the Linbury studio theatre, adjacent to the Royal Opera House and home to the Royal Ballet, to present the collection. By the time we arrived at the venue on the morning of the show, the production team were already erecting canvas hammocks, swinging high above the catwalk. Snow was going to fall softly for the duration of the show, but perfecting the flow of polystyrene flakes from above was proving difficult – we wanted a flurry, not a blizzard.

Backstage the make-up team had begun unpacking their huge suitcases of small products and arranging them in front of the mirrors, model-ready. Eugene Souleiman and his hair team were next door laying extension leads and unravelling their toolkits of hairdryers, straighteners and curling tongs, enough, I feared, to blow the electrics of the Opera House. Just then, I was called back on set; the principal dancer of the Royal Ballet had just popped down and wanted to meet me. She was beautiful, in a balletic bird-like way, and shyly she began to explain that she would like to offer her services – could she perhaps be in the show? As the fireworks started bursting in my brain, I calmly said, 'Thank you. Perhaps you can open it.' As the dancer promised to be back for the rehearsal and disappeared to find herself some black pointes, we hurriedly rushed to our studio to retrieve a duplicate look, a black tulle tutu, and started altering the dress – on the way back in the car. Meanwhile, the collection was being steamed and arranged on rails for each of the models: Jade Parfitt, Lily Cole, Jasmine Guinness, Yasmin Le Bon and Erin O'Connor. With this line-up the show had potential to stun.

The inspiration for this catwalk had been waiting in the wings for some time. The sketches of Léon Bakst, the designer for the Ballets Russes, seem to dance across the page as he captures the movement of each character, draped in textiles of exquisite detail and beguiling artistry. These, along with the sepia-tinted photographs of Nijinsky, Pavlova and Karsavina – the lead dancers of this itinerant dance troupe – have always attracted me. Launched in 1909 by their founder and director Sergei Diaghilev, the company brought a new aesthetic to the arts world, pirouetting its way across Europe and the Americas, fusing dance, music and design, creating fairy-tale escapism with a touch of the avant-garde.

Under the Svengali-like influence of Diaghilev, the Ballets Russes' productions become an artistic melting pot, an experiment in creative dynamics, the management of imaginative egos. And in the same way, by producing a collection and guiding it through to a catwalk presentation, the creative director nurtures the vision from concept to creation, bringing together complementary artistic forces so that they infuse and inspire.

The collection did not attempt to mask its 'Ballet Russes' inspiration. With stylist Deborah Brett we mixed a pale grey dancewear jersey into the collection and printed T-shirts with spirals of silvery swirling lines mimicking Bakst's fluid geometry and teamed them with satin slacks. Obvious tutu-shaped strapless dresses with sequinned contours, puffball satin mini-gowns topped with glitter-edged neck ruffs in icy blue and white and dresses with silk chiffon handkerchief-style skirts reminiscent of Pavlova's iconic costumes twinkled with crystal edging. Whitaker Malem, the leather-making design duo behind the armour of every sculptured superhero and gladiator in recent cinematic history, made bodices in tan and cream hides, which we matched with ballet pumps.

The bewitching soundtrack, the haunting score of Tim Burton's *Edward Scissorhands* by Danny Elfman, was the starting point for the show's music, and the vision of the models wandering through a snowy landscape inspired Souleiman to twist the models' hair with wire into horn-shaped sculptures and unicorn spikes, while Tilbury, whose mantra was, 'lips or eyes darling, you can't have both', painted on 'sticky' lips and nude eyes with a touch of mascara.

The show was about to begin. Backstage, the models huddled to chat, and in the dim shadowy light they appeared like mystical creatures getting ready to venture out into the night. As the magical snowflakes began to fall and the principal dancer took to the stage, en pointe, weightless and sylphlike, the adrenaline kicked in and sharpened my senses and as I looked towards the model line-up, I realised … this collection was really bad. Every other component – the models, hair, make-up, set, music and audience – was perfect, but somehow the styles had just drifted off course. I shuddered; my fate was sealed and I felt a cold front coming in.

Creative people are often thin-skinned, and we bruise easily. Judgement quickly sinks through to our veins and makes for the heart in an instant. While this sensitivity nurtures creativity, its flipside is pain. However, this vulnerability, which at times seems abnormal, unfathomable and unfair, is the life force for those of us who can fall in love in a moment and crumble with just a word.

One by one the models returned from the catwalk and I viewed each look with growing incredulity. The post-show party was a blur. As I attempted to dull my emotions with champagne, forcing myself to be bubbly to save face, I felt some guests were keeping their distance, while others feigned enthusiasm. But if Diaghilev himself had whispered congratulations into my ear, I would have scowled at him for lying to me.

The next morning, I forced myself to go to the local newsagents, hoping that the show hadn't made the papers. But as I scanned the lower shelves, I saw her on the front cover of the *Mirror*: Yasmin Le Bon wearing the crimson puffball and the headline...

Does my Bon look big in this?

Ultimately, it was a salutary experience. Such public humiliation is something I never want to experience again, and while I acknowledge that any creative endeavour will receive mixed reviews, I am more careful. For one season only, I had let my work fall into the lap of the British press's desire for 'funny fashion' to titillate the masses and sell copy. Strangely, though, the years have been kind to the collection. Perhaps the beauty of the unexpected snowfall and the almost supernatural charm of the styling has superseded the memory of the actual garments; for this, the show I most wanted to forget, has turned out to be the show that everyone else remembers.

A few years ago Alexandra Shulman, the then editor of British *Vogue*, was sitting in the front row of our show. I was thrilled; I liked Shulman; she had a brutal delivery that amused me and was intent on maintaining the old-fashioned behaviour of the fashion editors of yesteryear – the power to kill designers with a flick of her tongue. As an established designer, I occupy a strange place in the industry as far as the fashion press are concerned. No longer considered new or cutting edge, I miss out on their enthusiasm to nurture. But neither are we a big enough advertiser to be courted. At a cocktail party at the American consulate after the show, I asked Shulman for her thoughts on my collection. 'I liked the music,' she said.

> *Dear Alex, thank you so much for coming to the show and I am pleased you liked the music. It was intended to be upbeat and I did see you tapping your foot, on the monitor backstage – success! But really, four words for four months of my life! Was that a passive-aggressive comment? It was difficult to decipher really – as you probably did like the music but I get the feeling … that perhaps, it was the only thing you did like about my*

show, am I right? Oh dear, I wish we could have had longer to chat, but you seemed to be looking over my shoulder at someone else ...

The letters we write as we lie awake at night seem so much more articulate than what we might say at the time. Slipped into the mailbox of unsent retribution, they release our sense of injustice and in the morning our anger seems to have diffused. But in this case, the next morning, when I recalled Shulman's snappy critique, rather than agonising over her comment I found myself wondering why there is sometimes such a lack of sisterhood within the business of fashion. My show had been a celebration of women from beginning to end, and whether Shulman was right or wrong, her quip had been pure power play, a one-liner designed to make me wobble in my stilettoes.

It was Peggy Guggenheim, the art collector, bohemian, eccentric style queen and alleged nymphomaniac, who had started me thinking. A postcard of her had slipped out of a box as I tidied my shelves one day. Peggy was perched on the edge of a sunlounger against the backdrop of Venice's Grand Canal, her beloved Lhasa Apso dogs on her lap. Her eccentricity is obvious. 'Peggy ... you look so mad,' I said aloud as I picked up the card and studied it. She's wearing her famous butterfly-shaped sunglasses designed by

Edward Melcarth – clearly a surrealist accessory – but it's Peggy's rather glum, downturned mouth that makes the look so bizarre and reminds me of a Diane Arbus portrait, one of the many in which the subject seems deeply at odds with their chosen identity. I knew a bit about Peggy's life, and thought back to the last time I had visited the Guggenheim Collection in Venice, her home until her death in 1979. As I wandered through the palazzo's galleries of Pollock, Kandinsky, Giacometti and Miró, I became fixated on which of the exhibited painters and sculptors had become her lovers. Peggy's reputation for having lustful liaisons with her new-found talent is well known, but what had attracted Peggy first, the man or his art?

I was once at a college house party on a second date with a fine art student who had invited me to his room on the pretence of showing me his work. Canvases of mucky, unimpressive Impressionism were scattered around the walls and my heart sank in an instant. So I told him they were lovely and that I was going to get us some drinks, climbed out of the bathroom window and never saw him again. Our relationship was over before it began, my attraction wilting at the sight of his flaccid brushstrokes. Peggy had had better luck; with friends like Yves Tanguy and Marcel Duchamp, there would have been no excuse for her to leave so abruptly.

I find out more. Peggy opened her first gallery, Guggenheim Jeune in Cork Street, London, in 1937. A year on, she closed the gallery and moved to Paris, then, just a few days before the Nazi occupation, she smuggled her art collection, along with some of her artist friends, out of the city. Later, Peggy arrived in New York with her husband-to-be, artist Max Ernst, and together they created a new artistic space, the Art of This Century Gallery.

In 1943 the gallery hosted 'Exhibition by 31 women' – possibly the first ever women-artists-only show. The chosen, mostly surrealists, included Frida Kahlo, Dorothea Tanning and Peggy's own daughter, Pegeen Vail Guggenheim. In Peggy's autobiography *Out of This Century*, the exhibition is hardly mentioned; suffice to say it ended her marriage with Ernst. While out visiting the artists to collect their art, Ernst had fallen for 'Miss Tanning', who Peggy considered 'pretentious, boring, stupid, and vulgar and who dressed in the worst possible taste'. Peggy is also quoted as wishing it had been an 'Exhibition of 30 women'.

My adoration for Peggy was growing. I admired her courage and, as she said herself, she was a liberated woman long before there was a name for it. But it was the number '31' that stopped me in my tracks. My original idea for the collection had been to borrow Peggy's eccentric style and take inspiration from her collection of mid-century modern art. However, 31 was about the size of a collection. And then I had an idea: I would copy Peggy and have my very own exhibition of 31 women – a collection of dresses created for women whose personal style is/was inspirational – dead or alive. So, just like Peggy and her jury who had got together to select the artists for her gallery, my design team submitted their ideas and we argued each applicant's suitability.

The *Daily Mail* called our selection 'a motley crew of muses' and perhaps they were – amongst others we selected were Bardot, P.J. Harvey, Frida Kahlo, Béatrice Dalle, Charlotte Rampling, and even Peggy herself – but the brief had caught our imagination and, motley or not, we were inspired. We studied each woman's style, their chosen cut and colours and, by doing so, I was drawn into their lives – their careers, lovers and husbands. I listened to their music, watched their films and followed their art-collecting clues so that when, finally, my pencil hit the paper, I could design a gown worthy of its muse.

For Peggy, I designed a chiffon kaftan printed with the artist Alexander Calder's concentric circles stretched to fit the pattern. The gown seemed an apt homage to Peggy's distinctive taste, her iconoclastic waywardness and skilful intertwining of all business and personal matters. Kahlo's dress was ablaze with tangerine and fuchsia hues, Mexican blooms embroidered with an Impressionistic twist, and for P.J Harvey a pair of beaded, pinstriped palazzos worn with a nipple-flaunting lace blouse and dramatic wide-hemmed sleeves channelled her androgynous appeal.

Dita wore the dress I designed for her a few years later to a party in an aquarium: a mermaid-shaped gown with an underwired mesh bodice embroidered with a flower design stolen from a piece of 1930s jacquard weave. Meanwhile, the style inspired by Jennifer Connelly was worn by *Fleabag*'s Phoebe Waller-Bridge at the 2019 British Academy Television Awards, and it was Mandy Moore who graced the red carpet with the dress inspired by Julianne Moore – a red lace tulle sheath (not my intended target, but they had the same surname, and in any case Mandy wore the dress beautifully). And Grammy award-winning singer Janelle Monáe wore the style designed for Jennifer Lawrence to the 28th Palm Springs International Film Festival. Ultimately, it was a bit of a muse mix-up, a celebrity swap shop – but then again, not so unsuccessful.

Since then I have often played with random muse selection. To design a dress with universal appeal is almost impossible, so to imagine a particular woman who is easily accessible by way of their talent, style and fame focuses the creative mind and can add some diversity to the collection.

*

I am back in the warehouse and so busy daydreaming that I have hardly noticed someone had unzipped the bags behind me and was arranging the collections ready for me to view. Recently we have visited the archive to find inspiration, using it as a resource for the team, and, while I consider being able to enrich my creativity with my own body of work an accomplishment, I just wish I was able to untangle my memories from the gowns. Then again, as I move along the rail, I start to enjoy their richness and test myself by guessing the season each design belongs to, and where the collection was shown – London, Milan, New York or Moscow?

'Are you one of those designers who makes clothes nobody wants to wear?' said Prince Andrew. I feigned a smile and made a mental note to pen him one of those unsendable letters later that night. But more than anything I wanted to get away from him because at that very moment, just down the hall, a thousand Russians were waiting to see my show, my first at Russian Fashion Week, and there I was sipping champagne in a hospitality suite, frowning and speechless.

I may have felt more relaxed if, when I had gone back-stage a few minutes earlier, the models had been dressed in their first outfits, lined up and show-ready, the hair and make-up teams working the line, powdering the models' skin and teasing their curls. If that had been the case, I might have been inclined to challenge HRH. However, when I had left – or rather been pulled away and 'ordered' to attend the impromptu drinks reception – I was already panicking, frantically trying to find the models, who were last seen disappearing into the vast tented complex to show off their sparkly gowns to their friends and family.

Meanwhile, due to an outbreak of bird flu, our essential show kit – a box of backstage necessities and shoes for the show – had been impounded at the airport. Two young interpreters and a Fashion Week official had gone to the airport to 'sort things out', and I was left not only linguistically debilitated but shoeless too. Inside the 'seized' box, along with the needles, threads and some spare beads, were 'chicken fillets' (the nickname for those jelly-like pads used to put in bras to increase cleavage). Someone in our office had dutifully typed 'chicken fillets' on the customs forms and, understandably, the shipment had been stopped. The idea of raw bird flesh squashed between silvery slingbacks at the time of a poultry pandemic had quite understandably caused a bit of an incident.

It was Alexander Shumsky, a burly Russian bear of a man, who had invited us to Moscow to add a little international sparkle to his newly created Fashion Week, to launch the capital as the new destination for the fashion world's press and buyers. It was 2004, and the Russian boutiques had just become thirsty for some international fashion – the more glamorous the better – so we had leapt at the chance to recreate our latest London show with the intention of attracting a new customer – the Russian woman.

I extricated myself from the royal reception and headed backstage. The shoes had finally arrived, and I found the young interpreters giggling, recounting how they had enticed the customs officers into releasing the boxes by repeatedly clutching their breasts to explain the fillets. Meanwhile, the models had begun to reappear and were slipping into their shoes and getting into line. The lights dimmed and the show began.

Our catwalk shows are usually 12–14 minutes long and we book 18–20 models in order to have two to three girls on the catwalk at the same time, so most models will have at least one change and some two. The running order is like a puzzle, and the game is to shuffle the components – model, dress, shoes and accessories – to create a show that runs smoothly from a technical perspective without damaging the artistic vision.

The rule is to have at least eight models on the catwalk between each girl's change, which allows them two to three minutes to undress and dress into their next look and for the teams to smooth wayward hair and apply powder. The shoes are always the problem: we need to guess and order sizes months before the show and only during the casting a few days before do we discover that all of our favourite models are a size 41 – and we only have three pairs of those. Towards the end of the casting when shoes are limited, I often feel we are paying more attention to the size of the models' feet than anything else.

To start, I lay out photographs of each style and hang the collection on a rail. Then, with my stylist and team, we experiment to find the most exciting order for the silhouettes and colours by rearranging and deleting styles. This will become our running order. I try to open the show with an unexpected look, add a wake-up moment in the middle – a sharp contrast in colour or a print – and close with something so beautiful that the memory of it lingers long enough to ensure a good review. As the casting starts and the models begin to arrive, we pull out designs for them to try and ask them to catwalk the length of the room. But first I ask their name, age and where they are from, and am instantly reminded that these lofty ethereal beauties are just young women, often a long way from home, google-mapping their way between designers, hoping to be booked and sad when they aren't. 'Beauty is a form of genius,' said Oscar Wilde. 'It makes princes of those that have it,' he added, and I agree. I am the first to look for beauty in

anyone, but I bow to the models' divine symmetry, mesmerised by their elongated and sculpted features, and am
excited to dress them. However, for a show, it is their walk,
the sashaying sway as they surf the floor in teetering heels,
that attracts me. A confident, sensual stride and a noncha-
lant gaze can often transcend even their visual sublimity.

A show is a fleeting experience, where creativity should
absorb the audience to the point of distraction. The
soundtrack is therefore critical as it establishes the mood
and the way in which the models move. It can reflect the
designer's inspiration, or their desire to create interesting
layers of diverse influence. The show producer, who manages the running of the show, usually has about 20 minutes
of music, which he/she will edit as the show progresses so
that certain tracks can be synchronised with a colour
change or mood. And in case of any delay backstage – a
dress put on back to front or a snapped heel – there are
tracks to spare.

But in Moscow that night, the music just ran out. As the
models in their final looks left the darkness backstage for
the floodlit catwalk, instead of walking to the end of the
runway, standing for a few seconds and walking back, they
began to twirl, pose and jostle for the attention of the press
and a front row of oligarchs and bodyguards, flirting for a
few more minutes of fame than we had music. Amid the

silence I could hear the sticky tap-tapping of multiple stilettos on the catwalk's plastic covering, until the show producer pushed play and off they went again – from the beginning. Meanwhile, backstage without a monitor and oblivious to the show's new, freestyle choreography, I just waited with my team, wondering where the models had gone – once again!

In London or New York, the models' rebellion would have been viewed as a disaster, but at the time, Moscow was the fashion world's Wild West; it was lawless and anything seemed to go. The applause we received that evening was rapturous, and when the models did eventually return, they basked in an afterglow of adoration.

We continued to show in Russia for the next six seasons and began to supply the country's luxury retailers. The enthusiasm of the Fashion Week team, combined with the excitement of the Russian women at being presented with international designers, was intoxicating. The catwalks in Moscow were followed by press conferences and the after-show parties by hangovers, and separating our vodka-drenched dreams from reality became the brunch-time chat the day after. However, we cut short our adventures in Moscow after traces of plutonium were found on the upholstery of our return plane to London amid the ongoing investigation into the murder of

Alexander Litvinenko in 2006. With that my team's enthusiasm evaporated.

> *Dear Prince Andrew, it was so lovely to meet you earlier today, and a surprise! It is quite late now and I've had a few drinks at the after-show party, so I'll keep this short. Rather than answer the question you posed earlier today, I wanted to ask you, are you one of those princes who wears clothes nobody wants to wear?*

It is our first show at New York Fashion Week and a transparent tulle catsuit encrusted with vintage rhinestones is the first look. The model steps out against a painted antique-rose backdrop as a scratchy rapping rendition of Noël Coward's 'Mad Dogs and Englishmen' starts up, drowning out the nattering of the front row. Meanwhile, standing in the wings, I am both mad with excitement and feeling very much like an Englishwoman about to bare herself ...

Inspired by the decadence of the aristocratic and artistic elite of the 1930s, the collection, spring/summer 2011, reflected my own clichéd interpretation of an old English country garden party. Debutantes in pastel hues of luscious silks mingle on the lawn, coquettishly flirting with the eligible and notable, while a dapper Cecil Beaton plays paparazzi, capturing the social butterflies as they pose against walls of rosy blooms. The tinkling of the ivories and background birdsong muffle the haughty tones of their chattering. But as the champagne flows and the sun sets, the veneer of perfection slips and the party slides into a twilight tango between the tipsy couples. Then, as the bright young things begin to find each other totally irresistible, they trickle off, disappearing into the darkening bushes – 'makin' whoopee'!

I admit I was playing to the audience; I thought it would be foolish to ignore Americans' love of everything quintessentially British. Our decision to cross the pond was a commercial adventure to create more interest for the brand in the US. We had yet to clinch Neiman-Marcus – an important player in the gown market; we had their interest but not their orders. But that wasn't the only reason.

Rewind six months. I remember the moment exactly. It was 11.30pm and we were driving past Mornington Crescent tube station. We had just presented our latest collection, inspired – ironically – by the vibrancy of New York's early 1980s club scene, but instead of enjoying the anticipated rush of adrenaline, Mathew and I had found ourselves falling into a post-show slump.

'Well, that was a fucking disaster,' I said, 'I'm never going to show here again.' Mathew replied by slamming his foot on the accelerator and we sped home in stony silence. We had thrown everything at the show: a supercool and costly public relations company who had promised us a 'fabulous' front row, a techno band from Berlin, flown in to perform live and look edgy, and an abstract installation of mesmerising black and white optical patterning, a collaboration with the artist Anthony Burrill. Everything had been looking so great.

However, as show time approached, the front row was still conspicuously empty. 'Don't worry Jen, darling, they're coming,' the overfamiliar PR had shouted down the corridor to me. 'They're on the bus – last show started late – don't worry.' Meanwhile, as I fussed backstage, trying to stay calm and making last-minute checks of the first looks, the bus transporting the top-tier press and front-rowers had taken an abrupt turn and was now heading away from our venue towards the Burberry after-show party. I imagine that somewhere between Sloane Street and the Strand, what's-her-name, the fashion editor from the *Telegraph*, or the curly-haired one from *The Sunday Times*, had decided to call time: 'Jenny Packham's show or Burberry? Sequins or plaid? Hands up!'

I don't believe that 'things happen for a reason', but as we were left to hastily usher our friends and family into the front row (the ultimate seating plan failure), unbeknown to us, our fortunes had changed. A flickering green light had just begun to glow on the shore of Manhattan – more than 3,000 miles away.

Sometimes a bit of bad luck, personal humiliation, bitterness, anger, frustration and a few days of self-pity can eventually pay dividends. It is perhaps the way one reacts to a situation that gives it reason and so, having been forced to accept that our nicheness had become much of a muchness to the British press, we decided to use the difficulty and rather than dress up our gowns with 'techno dubstep' we sidestepped London Fashion Week altogether and took our show to a new audience – stateside.

There was a definite buzz around our first show in New York, but at the time, operating out of a photographic studio downtown, working late into the night casting models and styling the looks with the hair and make-up teams, I wouldn't have noticed a buzz if it had bitten me! Everything comes together in the last few days, and away from home, temporarily suspended from homework supervision and the school run, I could immerse myself in the collection, refining the details and experimenting with the running order, optimising every moment. The move to New York to show at the Lincoln Center had excited the design team, and the collection that season had evolved to take on a more confident and sophisticated aesthetic. It was more reflective of my values as a designer, and I no longer felt apologetic for presenting a collection of purely evening wear; the gown market in the American department stores is a serious business.

On the day of the show, after I took my bow, I waited anxiously in the wings to find out if I had managed to catch the imagination of my new audience. Had they come with me into my glamorous English garden party? These few moments after a show when I am left in the dark are always tense. Then, the big-shot buyers and the VIPs bustle backstage and I nervously watch the way they move. Do they push or pause? Are they eager to catch my gaze and smile? If so, I can relax. However, if they linger, hesitate and appear to be searching for the right words, the party is over.

Not long after, the actress Andrea Riseborough wore the collection's hand-painted floral shirt dress to a Warner Bros party, Emma Roberts the platinum beaded backless sheath at a premiere in LA, *Glee* star Jayma Mays looked pretty in peachy chiffon at the Screen Actors Guild Awards and Sandra Bullock showed off her new 'bangs' on the red carpet at the Golden Globes in a one-shouldered beaded tulle dress. The Duchess of Cambridge's first JP dress, a sequinned sheath, was worn to the ARK 10th Anniversary Gala, and her second, a short silk style printed with cloudy-coloured hydrangeas, was worn to a polo match in LA – both gowns were from this show.

Following our catwalk, the collection was featured on an episode of *Gossip Girl*. Guest actress Elizabeth Hurley strode across the screen – 'I'm off to the Jenny Packham fashion show,' she announced – and the next morning Neiman Marcus sent us their order. As they say, 'You wait for ages for one bus and then three come along at once!'

We showed in New York for the next eight years, building up our air miles and US customers' orders by taking advantage of New York's position as the first in the Fashion Week calendar, tempting the buyers to give us their dollars before globetrotting to London, Milan and Paris. But then, a few seasons ago backstage at our New York show, a model squeezed past me and everything changed. Her hair had been styled but it was sticking out in all the wrong places. I time-checked my phone; things were getting tight and I was anxious. The model and I needed to get to the hairstylist quickly, but I couldn't move for the bustling bunch of beauty press hustling for interviews. But that, after all, was the deal. In return for sponsoring our top artists, the hair and make-up brands got unlimited backstage access, but the problem was that backstage had become 'selfie central' and I needed some space. So I forced my way through the crowd and onto the catwalk, where the production crew were busy arranging metres of trailing plastic ivy around a polystyrene version of a crumbling wall, English-vicarage style, the backdrop to our show. It wasn't going well, and rather than looking lush and green, the ivy was sparse, wilting almost. The show was to be a homage to traditional British design – Scottish tartan, the East End's Pearly Kings and Queens, Aran sweaters, tweed – all styled up with an eighties twist. As the sound-check started and the first track played – Billy Bragg's signature ballad 'A New England' – *that* thought, the one that had been there for a while, the whisper that suddenly shouts above the noise, unexpectedly popped out: 'I'm done with showing in New York.'

The backstage chaos was indicative of the increasing power of social media. The clamour for images for Instagram and Snapchat had invaded the sanctity of the show's working environment; our compromise for sponsorship had tipped the balance. For me, the integrity of the show was being challenged and so, in the following seasons, our focus shifted towards producing photographic campaigns, released over Fashion Week and creating press events and private previews with the editors and influencers. Looking back, I had perhaps been suffering from show burnout. The relentless show routine had temporarily lost its allure for me, and its cost was no longer a convincing investment.

Alexandra Shulman once bluntly asked me, 'Why do you show? Your dresses look good on hangers.' I had winced at the time, but maybe she had a point. For a 'destination', niche brand without handbags and perfumes to promote, the straight-to-consumer-style show may have limited usefulness. But now, with the world at our fingertips and primed to receive 'Insta-shows', we can specifically target a potential clientele who have been captured by lifestyle and age through digital intelligence and send them our latest collections in an instant. This seems like a more sustainable, democratic approach, allowing a designer to go off-piste to create capsule collections between seasons, quickening the response to emerging trends, and to refresh and perfect their ideas. However, in the past to be perceived as a 'designer' demanded a show and while it is now just one of a myriad of options available to present a collection, the mystique of the old-style runway, the inescapable magic for the audience of 'being there', I must admit is difficult to replace.

And for me, nothing beats that moment when the show is about to begin, the models are in the line-up, their laughter fades and they become focused, stand taller and poised, their eyes sparkling with nervous excitement, the gowns pressed and perfect. Just then, and for a few seconds only, I am at the party that has yet to begin, floating in a bubble protected from the future and relieved of the past – truly in the moment. Then a sense of privilege consumes me (it's self-indulgent, I know): an awareness of how very luxurious it is to be able to create some kind of beauty, in the only way I know how, and then to set it free.

RED CARPET

Apparently, the Catholic cardinals were the first to roll out the red carpet. As early as the 1200s the 'crimson path' was a symbol of the cardinals' willingness to spill their own blood in God's name, or a manifestation of the blood of Christ. It all sounds a bit Monty Python to me – a cardinal popping into his local carpet shop asking if they have something available in the 'colour of Christ's blood'. I prefer to think they wanted a bit of razzmatazz in their day job – a desire to be worshipped for their sartorial splendour. I can visualise them now, decked out in their red cassocks, their gold chains with crosses, gently swinging up the aisle along with the burning incense on a bed of lush tufted scarlet, watched by an adoring crowd. I can imagine the swell of greatness, the feeling of empowerment that these ecclesiastical A-listers must have felt.

And so, unsurprisingly, the great and the good – and anyone who assumes themselves to be – have wanted their own red-carpet moment ever since, and this thin layer of flame-coloured fabrication has come to represent the rightful pathway of the successful, powerful, beautiful and rich on which to seduce their fans.

The pigment required to create scarlet was originally and for many centuries derived from the crushing of a tiny insect, the cochineal. An inhabitant of Central America, the cochineal lives on the nopal cactus leaf and is farmed by each insect being individually brushed off the plant by hand, dried and then pulverised, a painstaking task. Thus the dye became a much sought-after and valuable commodity, a colour with a waiting list, and the cloth dipped into this precious pigment became the exclusive tint for royalty, aristocracy and the religious elite. In the late 1800s, the innovation of synthetic dyes brought relief for the cochineal population and, at last, the general public could afford red and the colour of blood, passion and desire: the hue with the X factor became ours at last. And yet, despite its increased availability red has maintained its resonance, and its use as a backdrop for award ceremonies and royal occasions still stirs up a sense of occasion and excitement. So naturally, as a designer of glamorous gowns, the allure of dressing women for the red carpet captures my imagination.

I don't cry during films. If I do come close, I flip myself out of the drama, annoyed at being cajoled into the make-believe emotional turmoil, and by doing so strip away the mystique of the scene to avoid feeling sad. But it did happen once, during those tragic final moments of the 1997 epic *Titanic*. In the scene when Jack (Leonardo DiCaprio) slips away into the Atlantic's icy darkness, leaving Rose (Kate Winslet) clinging to a floating plank … yes, a tear (or two) did fall. Years later when I met them both, on different occasions, my moment of soppy simpering meant I felt a heightened sense of excitement about them.

I wouldn't say she looked scruffy, not exactly, but dressed as she was in a khaki jacket, faded jeans, ankle boots and her hair pulled back into a knotted bundle, it had taken me a moment to recognise the woman who had just slipped in through the door of our shop as Kate Winslet. With only a few hours' notice of her visit, I had dashed to Mayfair from my studio feeling unprepared. My hair was a mess and, in the taxi, I had plucked away the cotton threads and cat hairs from my jacket – I hadn't expected to meet an Oscar-winning icon that day. It was March 2012.

Winslet's visit was a surprise but it wasn't by chance. Earlier that year we had dressed her in a black and ivory satin gown with a softly twisted neckline for the Golden Globes. The dress had been a design from our 'Film Noir' collection and selected through our West Coast PR agency; it had been an exciting surprise wear. The press had loved the look. The *LA Times* had called the gown 'stunning in its simplicity' but more importantly remarked that it emphasised 'Winslet's statuesque beauty, giving her an almost regal, "I'm above playing the fashion game" air'.

To be able to place a gown on an A-lister is good, but for the actress to be universally complimented is a real success. But, how *does* a designer get a dress on the red carpet? For us, it had taken over a decade of sartorial social climbing to even begin to dress the world's leading ladies, and the only way to the top had been to edge our 'loans' – the dresses sent out to be worn to events – away from British TV stars in order to attract the majors – Hollywood film actresses and musicians such as Angelina Jolie, Emily Blunt and Taylor Swift. This strategic move had sent us into the wilderness for a few years – to be rediscovered, we needed to be forgotten. This was painful, but without elevating our brand by dressing a clientele of film stars, we would be unable to capture and support our desired retail partners and grow our business. So, with our sights set on the American market, we took the collection to LA to entice the top stylists towards our gowns by inviting them to our suite at the Chateau Marmont for an exclusive viewing.

It soon became apparent that the life of a celebrity stylist is not as easy as I had imagined. Working in a maelstrom of egos, dancing between designers and their clients to gratify the film production companies' need for their star to shine the brightest while dodging the sharp-shooting snipes of the fashion press, the stylists strive to create a moment of fashion history for their client by composing a 'look' of timeless glamour with an unexpected spin, dressing them with the confidence to step out before the world and beguile. And just like me, a stylist's success, their ability to catch an A-lister and dress her is enhanced by the clients they already have and how well and long they have dressed them. It's a chicken and egg situation.

After each collection is shown, images are immediately sent out to the stylists and the collection is flown to the LA office for their clients' fittings. Alternatively, the stylists or even the celebrity will contact us directly. And occasionally, a celebrity will go shopping and buy one of our dresses themselves for an event.

At the Golden Globes in 2016, Bryce Dallas Howard told the E! Red Carpet reporter that she had bought her

Jenny Packham gown, a navy sequinned maxidress with a plunging lace-filled décolleté, from her local Neiman Marcus store because 'I like having lots of options for a size 6 (UK size 10) as opposed to maybe one option.' The press was overwhelming. Bryce brought attention to the shocking fact that most designer collections available to them are a UK size 6 or 8 (mine included) and at the same time won points for being brave enough to admit that her dress was 'off the rack'.

By the way, I have never paid to place a dress, and even if I had the budget to do so, I'm not sure I would. That's cheating, isn't it? As the luxury design houses pay to place their designs on the stars, the fashion industry mutters 'paid placement' as if it doesn't really count, but to the audience these payments are irrelevant and the game goes on. However, after a while the stylists feel thwarted by their lack of choice and then the red-carpet catwalk begins to lose its sizzle as the element of surprise fizzles out. Yes, there is a touch of indignation in my words. As the crimson carpet is rolled out from one award night to another until its shade deepens into the 'exclusive', almost burgundy tone of the most famous carpet in the world – the lush high pile of the Oscars – the chances of being included diminish as the big brands flex their muscles and the rest of us are elbowed out. But then again, it makes waking up in the night to a vibrating phone as a star steps out in one of our dresses even more of a buzz.

I am not usually dazzled by celebrity, but this time it was different. This was Kate 'wondrous' Winslet, my favourite actress, and I can remember bubbling up with excitement at the prospect of dressing her, so I swiftly disconnected from the 'relationship' I'd imagined I had with her from watching her on screen so that I wouldn't be tempted to spout such silliness as, 'Is DiCaprio a good kisser?' – which had popped into my head as I began to pull out styles from the new collection to show her.

I needed to appear cool. This was a chance for me to dress an actress who entranced me with her screen presence. She was top of my must-dress list and I was prepared to pull out all the stops – and I was going to need to because, for this dress, the one she would wear to the Albert Hall premiere of *Titanic 3D*, I had just four days. A dress of this kind would normally take much longer to make – from sketch to dress, weeks, possibly even months. It was Thursday, the premiere was on Sunday – and I had no idea how I was going to do it.

Luckily, this was to be an unusual collaboration. Winslet would be in town in the lead-up to the premiere and available for a fitting. To be able to have just one fitting, let alone an interaction, with a celebrity client is rare, even with a bespoke piece. Given the importance of this event, I was surprised there wasn't already a gown 'in the bag' hanging in her hotel room. Perhaps there had been another dress in the making that hadn't worked out and I could come to the rescue: all I needed to do was tempt Winslet with my collection and get her to trust me to make something beautiful.

To make something beautiful – what does that really mean and what makes a good red-carpet dress? For a stylist it is about finding the dress that accentuates their client's beauty and style, enough to grab our attention and inspire us and by doing so create the whirl of publicity the film industry desires. The pale-yellow Valentino gown worn by Cate Blanchett at the 2005 Academy Awards springs to mind. The one-shouldered taffeta style with an A-line skirt draped into a pleated backed train, cinched at the waist with a chocolate ribbon, was a true Hollywood starlet dress. Pitch perfect against Blanchett's golden blonde curls and milky complexion, and with a dash of poppy red lipstick, the look is unforgettable for its freshness and ... beauty.

Blanchett's dress is a perfect example of dress and woman combining to form an elegant, aesthetic equality. It is important that the dress catches our imagination but doesn't distract us from the actress. However, I couldn't imagine a design that could possibly compete with Winslet's radiance and vitality – to describe her I would use the word 'Alive'. Some people really do seem more aware of the true reality of the human existence – that it is nothing more than just a blip, on a dot, in the black mass of the universe – those who imagine each moment as one lost rather than one less to live. Winslet's energy was effervescent.

My project notes for this dress were coming together. *Titanic 3D* was being released in the centenary of the disaster. In 1997, when the original film had first been shown, my grandmother, Betty, had not been impressed with the story's glamorous Hollywood makeover. The sinking of the *Titanic* had rocked Southampton, and her childhood memories of the collective grief felt for the city's 540 lost crew members still resonated. Therefore, intuitively, I thought the dress should not be flippant in colour or detail and, given that Winslet would be the focus of attention at this event, the star and, in my mind, the fictional sole survivor of the terrible tragedy – Rose DeWitt Bukater – re-emerging 15 years later, the dress needed some gravitas. Perhaps Winslet understood this too; she wanted the dress to be black.

By the time she left an hour later, I had in my mind the silhouette of the dress, the fabric and the essence of what she was after. Our challenge now was to make it. With a second appointment at her hotel already arranged, we scribbled up some designs in the taxi on the way back to the studio and soon we were pulling out rolls of fabrics and checking our stocks for something beautiful that would work.

Early on Saturday morning we arrived at Winslet's hotel in Covent Garden. We waited for her in the adjoining room and I checked out the hotel's contemporary cosy décor, with its dark walls and lively printed cushions. When she was ready, Kate slipped into one of the toiles we had made overnight – a black stretch crêpe gown with a plunging neckline. We had a backup style too – a scarlet dress with a slash neck – but as soon as she tried on the black, we knew it was the one.

My head pattern cutter and official 'VIP Fitting Accomplice', Simon, then nipped and tucked the dress while Winslet kept a watchful eye on her reflection in the mirror. Connoisseurs of the red carpet, especially actresses, are aware of themselves in a way that most of us choose not to be, and take their time to perfect their look. To be red-carpet ready really means being prepared to be scrutinised by the world's press, who will sharpen their focus on your every angle, bulge and wrinkle. Winslet is a professional and knows only too well that every detail is crucial, from the curvature of the seams to the swoop of the neckline. During the appointment she shared with us a trick for how to create cleavage without wearing a bra or adding boning; by attaching some wide strips of ribbon, sewn into each armhole seam and then held taut, cupping the bust on either side and then secured into the under-bust seam – giving lift and pushing the breasts together – and it works. However, in most fittings for this kind of dress, I am asked for it to be made 'as tight as possible' – often so tight that the fabric strains at the seams and the zip's teeth chatter. Every millimetre seems to count and occasionally a gown can become irreparably broken. As the star slides sideways into their limo en route to an event, the zip splits and the back of her dress yawns wide open, unable to withstand the increasing pressure as the body spreads into a sitting position. This is one reason why there is always a backup dress.

Winslet's gown was looking good, tight but not about to split, and the alterations were minimal. We still needed to decide on the beading detail, so on the way back to the studio we took a detour to our press office to pick out a few styles with the intention of dismantling them and recommissioning their crystal embellishment.

In the sample room, three machinists worked that evening to finish the dress ready for the final fitting, one sewing up the lining, another unpicking and re-embroidering the beaded panels and a third putting everything together, while Simon fastidiously checked the pieces against Winslet's dress dummy. I just hung around making everyone anxious, nervous about the levelling of the skirt as it had to be hemmed to the millimetre so that it skimmed the floor perfectly. Hemming is usually the last process before a dress is completed and, if we are working to a deadline – which is often the case – mistakes can happen, scissors can slip and a dress with a hem that is even a little short can lose its drama.

It was the day of the premiere, and on the way into town the next morning, we were informed that Winslet had moved from the Covent Garden Hotel to Claridge's so, with the finished dress and our 'fit kit' – a box of pins, a needle, some thread and a few spare beads – we hotfooted it across town for what we hoped would be our final fitting. However, Winslet had not yet seen the dress completed with its new sparkly additions and I was on edge – would she like it?

Claridge's is one of my favourite places. I haven't stayed there, but I have had a cocktail in the bar, some soft little sarnies and dainty scones in the tea room and a few fashion shows in the ballroom. It is London's art deco landmark and a go-to hotel for the British and international elite

– film stars, designers and royalty. So it wasn't a surprise that Winslet had checked in. With the premiere now just hours away, things were obviously stepping up and this time when we knocked on the door it was answered by Winslet's publicist. After eyeing us up and spotting the dress bag draped over Simon's arm – and very likely our shattered demeanours – she guessed we were 'the dress people'.

'Can you wait here?' she said firmly, ushering us just inside the door and leaving us in the corner of what appeared to be a large suite. We felt like a couple of tradesmen, which in reality is exactly what we were – trading our creative services for a celebrity endorsement. Tit for tat. And in that moment I was feeling a bit like the tat.

The suite was luxurious and elegant, with high ceilings decorated by chandeliers of crystal droplets and 1930s-inspired chairs covered in silvery chenille. The rooms were busy with women dressed in black weaving between the furniture, either on their phones or making notes on clipboards; one or two of them just stood by with their arms folded, watching. I knew what was coming; it was going to be a public fitting with a judge and jury and there was a chance I would be found guilty of designing a dress 'unfit for purpose'. But just as my anxiety began to take hold,

Winslet appeared, beautiful in a black, sharply shaped suit, stiletto heels and her hair twisted into a chignon, smiling. She was doing some interviews and would be a few minutes more: did we want a cup of tea, she asked.

As the fitting began in the bedroom, nobody uttered a word as we slowly unzipped the dress bag and revealed the dress. As I unfastened the gown ready for Winslet to try, you could have heard a pin drop. After I had hooked the eye at the back of the gown, I glanced over Winslet's shoulder at her reflection in the wardrobe mirror – 'not guilty' shouted a voice in my head. The dress, or more accurately, Winslet in the dress, looked good, very good. There was a united sigh of relief.

The red carpet poured out from the entrance of the Royal Albert Hall, flowing down the steps before spreading out into a large scarlet puddle, the Victorian architectural epic towering in the background. It was a bright spring evening and long shadows cut across the walkway, creating waves of reddened tones as the stars and film-makers walked and talked, hugging, air-kissing and shaking hands.

I was there, too, on the other side of the roped-off arena, waiting with the crowd for the protagonist to arrive. We had been given tickets for the film screening but this was the big event, catching sight of the famous and successful before they all disappeared into the darkness to watch the *Titanic* sink once again – this time in 3D. Just then, the photographers began to surge towards the front of the carpet. Camera flashes began to pop, illuminating the crowd as they stood on tiptoe, eager to catch a glimpse: Winslet had arrived.

I never assume a dress is going to be worn – there have been too many disappointments along the way. I know what happens because I do it too. I have a dress waiting in my bedroom, shoes, a clutch bag and jewellery, and I relax, soaking in my bathtub, enjoying my 'getting ready' time. It is a perfect outfit; I even know the shade of lipstick I will wear. Twenty minutes before the taxi arrives, I zip up the dress, slip into the heels and clip on the earrings. I'm ready. I look in the mirror – and then I get changed. Somehow my mood and the 'look' have become discordant, and I feel uncomfortable. Panic ensues as I try out new combinations and fling my discarded skins about the room. Mathew waits in the street for the taxi, just as I declare, 'I have absolutely nothing to wear.'

This wouldn't happen if I had a stylist, of course, because they would know that the nearer the event, the more acutely we look into the mirror at ourselves, and so alternatives must be ready to cater for these moments of fashion fallout.

*

I saw her golden hair first, parted on one side and pinned up into a sleek retro forties-style bob, the cherry lips and her sparkling smile, and then the reassuring glimpse of a silvery sleeve and a dash of black – she was wearing the dress!

Winslet's gown was one of the most sustainable I have ever made. The fabric, a heavy silk crêpe, was woven in Italy and uncovered in our studio – we found we had eight metres left on the roll, which was exactly what we needed. The short sleeves, a hand-beaded cluster design of transparent crystals and Swarovski stones, had been stolen from a style from the previous season, and the centrepiece, a horizontal diamond-shaped motif made of metallic rings wound with silver, was found in a drawer in our beading archive. We neatened its fraying edges and added some large clasped crystals. A completely recycled dress.

When I was pregnant with my second daughter I decided to try hypnosis for pain relief in childbirth, and visited a practitioner in Bloomsbury. At my first session, sitting comfortably surrounded by cushions and covered with a mohair blanket, I closed my eyes and swiftly succumbed to the therapy.

'Imagine you are in a field. It's a beautiful day and you are feeling a soft breeze on your face. You are running your hands through the tall grass,' she said. This was all good; I liked being in the field.

'Now you see a child in the distance,' she continued in her slow melodic voice. So I visualised my older daughter running towards me. Then she said: 'This is you as a young girl. You are going to talk to her now.'

The tears came, quickly turning into heavy sobs as the image of my daughter morphed into me, aged seven.

In my subconscious mind, I was wearing the cornflower-blue velvet dress my mum had made for my Silver Medal ballroom dancing examination in the local church hall. It had leg-of-mutton sleeves, created by gathering the sleeve head into a puff and cutting to taper towards the wrist. However, the sleeve was too tight around my elbow and, as the pianist began to play and I reached up to hold the examiner's hands, the armhole ripped. Meanwhile, my white cotton lace tights were refusing to stay up, the gusset creeping down my thighs and my waltz was rapidly turning into a quickstep as I tried to keep my tights up by taking smaller and quicker moves!

I don't believe my tears can be explained by this early style-over-functionality trauma, and I have forgiven my mum; velvet is such a nuisance to sew – it slips and slides and the seam allowance goes rogue. So there was no obvious reason for this reunion to have been quite so emotional.

But at the same time, why wouldn't it be? In the midst of my busy life, I had forgotten my seven-year-old self and all the little sparks she had ignited – the dreams, and the waltzes she had danced for me.

How Winslet felt watching herself on the big screen, a young actress on the verge of international stardom, I have no idea, but there was an awareness I remember that the press were likely to compare her with her younger self, the 'then and now' photos side by side. Winslet's look that night reflected her rise to stardom and the retro styling was a throwback to the Golden Age of Hollywood, which aligned her rightfully with the great screen stars of yester-year. It was a look that would undoubtedly have impressed her 21-year-old ego.

So, what would *you* wear if you could have that moment, face to face with yourself at an age before you knew how things would be and what you would become?

How would your transformation be mirrored in your appearance? I think this is a challenging hypothetical question, and even as I contemplate the styling for such a rendezvous, myriad thoughts that go beyond the superficiality of 'what to wear' bubble up.

'When I was young I always used to imagine myself wearing a very long, green trench coat and red lipstick, and it always strikes me that when I wear anything approximating this, it does pop into my mind that my younger self would be pleased!' remarked a colleague when I asked her what *she* would wear.

Both the immediacy of her reply and its definitiveness surprised me, and I became intrigued by the concept that our choice of dress for this impossible reunion might be symbolic of our secret sense of identity. I began trawling images of the trench-coat-wearing icons – Catherine Deneuve, Audrey Hepburn, Sophia Loren – and then an image of Marlene Dietrich scrolled up. Smouldering in a dark, tightly tied version of the trench, with a power pout of ruby-coloured lips, her stylish look, a screenshot from the film *A Foreign Affair* (1948), seemed to match my idea of the style my colleague was after. However, Dietrich's character and style in the film seemed at odds with my colleague's gentle persona; the plot's protagonist, Erika Von Schlutow, a cabaret singer and a woman of intrigue known for her infamous collection of lovers, is a femme fatale extraordinaire. But even so, the image caused a subtle shift in my assessment of my colleague's character. Whether it was the correct interpretation of her look or not, an air of mystery began to swirl and this glimpse into the psyche confirmed how very little I may actually know of her.

To meet my younger self I would want to look 'grown up', elegant, graceful and groomed – the best red-carpet version of myself. I would have a manicure, a blow-dry, and spend time refining my eyebrows and flicking my eye-lashes with my most voluminous mascara. I would apply a smudge of Chanel lipstick and drench myself in my favour-ite perfume – Carnal Flower by Frederic Malle, a scent created from 'lustful tuberose'. High heels, definitely, and my most sparkly jewels – she would like those – and maybe I'd wear something black with a power shoulder and a touch of cleavage: glamorous, confident; and, even though I wouldn't expect her to take me seriously, I'd want my little self to say – Wow!

'From its origins, glamour has been associated with dream-ing.' This quote from Stephen Gundle's book *Glamour: A History* beautifully bypasses the confusing rhetoric around what being 'glamorous' really means. It is simply the stuff of dreams, the fashion fantasies of a younger self or our desire to dress up and suspend grown-up realities for an evening. And so, the spectacle of the red carpet arouses our senses and we imagine what it must be like to have a 'better', more perfect life as we watch the attention-seeking few who spin the story as they do their turns, dazzling us with their vibrancy, convincing us that transformation is possible.

I have dressed many of the world's most beautiful, charismatic and talented women, including Helen Mirren, Millie Bobby Brown, Uma Thurman, Reese Witherspoon, Oprah Winfrey, Adele, Cameron Diaz and Halle Berry. Red-carpet dressing is not limited by age or dress size and I pride myself in the diversity of our clientele. Glamour can be created and cultivated by all of us to enhance our own personal sense of style, and its empowering effect can boost our self-esteem. In lavishing ourselves with a touch of glitz we too can sparkle.

Oh no! I have my arm around Leonardo DiCaprio. I'm not sure how this happened: a few moments ago I was standing over the other side of the ballroom. But now I can feel the texture of his suit against my fingers and I think the tip of my stiletto is touching his toe but I'm too scared to look.

In his essay 'Speed' Oliver Sacks writes: 'There have always been anecdotal accounts of people's perception of time when they are suddenly threatened by mortal danger.' Then he quotes Albert Heim: 'Time became greatly expanded. In many cases there followed a sudden review of the individual's entire past.' Apparently, there is often an accompanying feeling of helplessness, passivity and dissociation.

And although I wasn't in mortal danger, as I sidled up to DiCaprio my emotions seemed to be mimicking a near-death experience. As everything slowed down, a rapid review of DiCaprio's acting highlights started rolling and suddenly I am standing next to Arnie Grape, Calvin Candie, Howard Hughes, Jordan Belfort, Amsterdam Vallon and Jack Dawson. But this multiple personality shuffle is too confusing, so I flip to having an out-of-body experience, dissociate and begin to watch myself – with embarrassed disbelief.

It is January 2014 and I am at the BAFTA Tea Party at the Four Seasons Hotel in Beverly Hills. I have been invited to the Golden Globes and this party is one of the many film industry get-togethers leading up to the big event. The room was buzzing when we arrived; Tom Hanks, Cate Blanchett, Sandra Bullock and Chiwetel Ejiofor lined the red carpet, getting snapped by the press, while in the ballroom the directors, producers and BAFTA team mingled, hedging their bets on the year's award nominees. It was the year of *Captain Phillips*, *Blue Jasmine*, *12 Years a Slave* and *The Wolf of Wall Street*.

I had broken the ice chatting with Blanchett, and on being introduced to Benedict Cumberbatch I had blurted out that we were neighbours – I'd spotted him on the Heath, I said. This is why I don't like approaching random 'famous people' and usually pretend I haven't seen them – it must be so annoying having to suffer such banal remarks.

Then, just as we were leaving, my colleague Blaire said, 'Look – it's Leonardo DiCaprio over there.' I followed her gaze towards a small ring of people in the centre of the room circling DiCaprio. And then – honestly – everything else is a blur.

I remember thinking, this is taking too long; my arm was beginning to ache and was slipping lower down his back. We had broken through the courteous gap left by the other guests and accosted him on either side. 'Can we get a picture with you, Mr DiCaprio?' I said. But he didn't flinch; he must have been used to this kind of bad behaviour and consciously took his time. I put this down to his collected coolness rather than a punishment, but as the slow seconds passed, I began to have that *Titanic* feeling – I was sinking, into an abyss of shame. And then he looked up and the picture was taken.

I was bemused by my behaviour that day and couldn't look at the photograph, the one of DiCaprio and me, for about six months. A severe sudden attack of Hollywood intoxication had caught me unawares and I had transformed from an international designer to fangirl in a split second. In that bizarre moment, the magnetism of the industry that offers escapism had felt like entrapment. The allure of the red carpet is so powerful that the stars who are brave enough to walk it have become the cardinals of our age. Our attention is captured by their otherworldly aura and we want to get closer and be doused in their perceived glory.

Whatever. It's a great photo.

AFTER-SHOW PARTY

'I'm sorry Jen,' he said, 'you've caught me with my trousers down.'

For a moment I was confused, imagining my dad in the hallway holding the telephone with his trousers crumpled around his ankles. Then he added: 'It's Mum, she's gone.'

'Where?' I said.

She had left that morning, waved goodbye to my dad and driven away to take her partially sighted friend to a hospital appointment. On the way, a catastrophic rupture of her aorta brought sudden death and my mum and her car came to an abrupt halt on the verge of a dual carriageway. Fortunately, no one else was hurt.

That evening, I moved through the rooms of my parents' home in dumb shock, taking notes on a life interrupted, searching for the clues that would help me

237

understand my mum's disappearance. The to-do list on the kitchen shelf – 'buy cake, pick up Dulcie – hospital' – two mugs, side by side, a spoonful of coffee and two of sugar in each, the knitting needles tucked down the side of the sofa, a hairbrush left on the bed, the everyday ordinariness of my mum's life, once unremarkable, had become enthralling.

In the darkened dining room, a small plastic bag glinted on the table. I hesitated for a moment, then reached out. A soft jangle of metal rolled against my touch and glowed golden in my palm.

'The police brought them,' said my dad from behind me. 'When they turned up this morning. They were young nippers,' he added.

Since I was young, my mum's love of trinkets, and in particular her rings, had charmed me, and I would play with them, twisting them around her fingers as she chatted, sharing their stories. Lying on the bed, she would weave her hands above us and I would follow the sparkle of her solitaire as it caught the morning sunlight and once more she would tell me about a boy up the road who went to sea and came back home to marry her.

My mum's rings lay heavy in my hand; the thin layer of plastic seemed to be the only protection between me and reality. And then, for a moment, I felt her arms wrap around me, the familiar compression and the waft of hairspray, and I knew: she was gone.

Relationships are formed by interaction – mutual interests, shared moments and time – and slowly, love weaves its way into our lives. For my mum and me, our passion for creating and decorating the world in which we lived was the constant thread that ran the length of our time together and, as I got to know her, I came to recognise that the act of 'making' was, for her, a multifaceted method of survival.

Her name was Rita and her story always started with the night the bomb landed on the air raid shelter. 'There was a big flash,' she would tell us, and my brother and I would pretend to yawn and fall to the floor, pleading 'not the bomb story again' as if it were just another rerun of a Grimms' fairy tale.

Over and over again, as the dust settled and the German plane flew home after scattering its lethal load over Southampton, my mum crawled out from beneath the shelter and stood in the rubble of her home, aged six.

Before helplines and Prozac, perhaps it was studious diversion through hobbies that brought some relief to a traumatised generation who grew up in a war, because my mum never stopped distracting herself, compulsively creating, every day. The 'doing' was everything and the end result was just more clutter. She wasn't precious about her efforts – just a quick acknowledgement from us and then she was on to the next project.

In every corner of our little house, her works in progress were scattered; sculptures, paintings, part-made dresses and half-stitched knits. She learnt Russian and played the harp and electronic keyboard, bred canaries and wrote poetry and short stories. She sang in a choir, played in amateur dramatics and at Christmas stuck candles onto logs with plasticine, sprinkling them with festive glitter to make the quickest-selling table decorations at the school fair. She fashioned tiny clothes for my dolls, threw together fancy-dress costumes and embroidered my pillowcases with Alice in Wonderland and the Mad Hatter. And the icing on the cake? A duck-billed platypus for my brother and Marie Antoinette for me, raising the bar for celebratory confectionery in the community.

So when I am asked, 'When did it all start?' I reply, 'Oh, I missed that bit. The party had already started when I turned up.'

Every few weeks, my mum and I would go on a remnant hunt in the local department store. It was just like Grace Brothers from the 1970s sitcom *Are You Being Served?*, complete with a gang of Mrs Slocombe lookalikes who would fuss about behind the glass-topped counters with their bouffant hairdos and powdery complexions. The shop seemed out of place on the high street, beginning to slip out of time as the newfangled retail trends of the early seventies, self-service and the insurgence of catalogue purchasing came along. It smelt like a second-hand bookshop, dusty and slightly damp, and was lit by flickering fluorescent strips and sprayed liberally with lavender scent. However, its pretensions set it apart – it felt 'posh'.

First, we would peruse the rolls of fabric stacked upright in the haberdashery corner, the cotton florals and gingham checks, crisp and starchy; then there were the wools, soft and spongey, and gradually we would edge our way towards the lurex and velvet, caressing their exotic textures and cooing in unison as if we had just stumbled across the crown jewels in a dustbin. My mum probably didn't want to be seen to be aiming straight for the remnants, so we would linger a while around the fancy trims and the button rack before casually strolling over to the offcuts.

Remnants are small pieces of fabric at the end of a roll. Too small for a retailer to keep attached, they are folded and put into a bucket-type display and sold at a discount. But it wasn't *just* their reduced price that made them attractive, it was the eclectic way they were thrown together, all higgledy-piggledy, creating a melee of exciting clashes of colour and texture. After we had rummaged, and ummed and aahed for a while, we would choose our favourites, hide them at the bottom of the pile and go upstairs, through the ladies' hat department and into the store's wondrous wicker-furnished tea room. There, as we buttered our toasted teacakes, my mum would open her notebook and together we would dream up designs to match the yard count of our treasure.

Later, as I cut my panels from the fabric on the backroom table, my mum would be on her knees on the floor, catching pins on her skirt as she circumnavigated her own layout, snipping around the pattern pieces. Then we would sit opposite each other and whizz up our styles, the whirring of our machines eclipsed by Bonnie Tyler and Rod Stewart spinning us a yarn from the turntable.

Inevitably, as I became a teenager and started to prefer my own designs, and as the usual mother–daughter conflicts began, my fight for independence would manifest itself through my rejection of the clothes she would so lovingly create for me. One day, an accident involving a chestnut-brown needlecord jumpsuit became the last straw and never again would I endorse a Mum-made garment. At the school bus stop I put my foot down and scissored my legs into a handstand, but before I hit the wall the design's low-slung crotch ripped wide open. My peep-show party trick and the ensuing laughter from my bus stop buddies determined that this would be the last gymnastically pro-pelled movement of my life and, in that splitting second, I sacked my mum from being my designer and accepted that perhaps the time had come to keep my legs together. It had to happen; our sense of fashion and preference of cut had – literally – grown apart.

'Look at these,' she said.

'Hang on,' I replied, busy searching for a thong, on my knees looking through the bottom rack.

'Come on, look,' she said and, when I turned, I could see her shoulders were already shaking; she was revving up, tittering to herself.

'These are no good, are they?' Her giggle had really got going now and she could hardly get her words out.

'Well, it depends what you're using them for, Mum,' I said cockily.

She was holding a pair of crotchless knickers by the hanger, poking her hand repeatedly through the hole, the missing bit. It was silly, but we couldn't stop. It was hysteri-cal in that wonderful way when your inhibitions stand back and say, 'Over to you – I'm out of here.' My mum was trying to tell me something about the knickers being sinful – not very 'hol-e-y' – and as we made our way towards the door, I slammed the thong on the counter and managed to splutter an inarticulate 'sorry' to the shop assistant and we left.

We never talked about sex – ever. Well, just the once, when she told me sex was dirty. An ambiguous description, I thought. We were always mother and daughter, she wasn't my friend, but in a lingerie department we were united by a common affection for 'unmentionables'. However long we browsed the rails, the discrepancies in both our age and outlook were suspended and we became two women enjoying a bit of luxury retail escapism, titillated and seduced by lacy loungewear, beautiful silky cupped bras and feathery tassels.

I tend to wear my heart on my sleeve, while my mum had stitched hers firmly into the lining of her pocket. We had our differences, but essentially we were cut from the same cloth. As life unfolded, as it does, creased and rarely ironed out, we were both inclined to pin our hopes on the transformative powers of a piece of fabric and a touch of imagination.

I started to erase my mum from the house shortly after her death, a few hours after I had arrived that evening. In the bathroom, I collected up her jars of skin cream and make-up and put them into a plastic bag. The kids would be arriving the next day and it might upset them, I had said to myself. Anything partly used became especially important to hide away because it meant that she had been in the process of doing something, which, in my state of shock, I just couldn't countenance.

Between then and the funeral, I cleaned every room, tidying up after her, trying to dust away the darkness that swept through me. And always in my mind was the wardrobe. It had been purchased when my parents moved into the house in 1963 and had formed part of a bedroom set of his and hers closets, a bed and dressing table. I had spent my childhood pulling out looks, posing and remodelling her clothes with safety pins, playing dress-up with strings of beads and scarves, stomping up to the mirror 'Dig in the dancing queen'.

I was born in that room and it crossed my mind that the wardrobe was maybe one of the first things I ever saw – all blurry and brown. But for now I kept my distance. In my sad madness, I imagined that behind its doors the full force of my loss was waiting to be released.

I want to climb in, curl up and tuck myself into one of its corners. Would that be so weird? To fold up my legs and snuggle into the wardrobe, close the door and shroud myself in the clothes, inhaling that musky scent of 'Eau de Mum' for one last time?

I glance up. My 13-year-old daughter is sat on the bed, her eyes locked onto me, and my dad is stood to my side, 79 years old, busying himself by unravelling the roll of black plastic bin bags. I notice that we have formed a triangle, the polygonal shape with most resistance and strength, and I think they may have guessed that I am drowning in grief. They are staring at me and I know what they are up to: they are trying to use their superpower of unconditional love to hold me up.

So we are doing this together? Yes, of course. I have no right to 'own' this moment, to have it to myself; but I feel I do. This process of 'sorting' her wardrobe is surely *my* domain, not theirs. I just want them to PLEASE go away and leave me alone ... with her ... clothes.

On reflection my coping strategy was regrettable, but at the time it was beyond my control to adjust my behaviour, and surely to criticise oneself for putting up some protection when the safety nets have fallen is unfair. To magic away a mother takes more than a spray of Flash and a hoover. There is no quick-fix clean-up that can remove the hard-to-shift stains of deep, ingrained affection.

I would use the word 'brutal' to describe the way I flung out her clothes.

Carefully, I unfastened the buttons on one of her hand-crafted jackets and reached inside, pulling out bus tickets, shopping lists and bits of tissue – the ubiquitous contents of a 76-year-old woman's pockets – and I held them in my hands, the heartbreaking remnants. Then, I began neatly folding her clothes, each and every item, stacking them into the bin bags, squeezing out the air as I knotted the tops. I thought that if it all went away, so would the pain. If I tied the plastic bin bags tight enough, I could suffocate the life out of this death.

Within the first few hours of life, we wriggle our tiny hands into the small sleeves of softly knitted cardigans and spread our toes into newborn booties with the help of our parents, feeling the smooth first fibres of babywear, and our relationship with texture begins. Later, as we grow, we begin to dress ourselves, evolving an identity. We update and edit our looks while adapting our wardrobes to suit our changing lifestyles and advancing age – until at last, we fall out of fashion and into death. And then, once again, someone dresses us.

The psychology of what we wear and how it influences those around us seems never more pertinent than after we give up the ghost. So I decided to dig deeper and caught up with my friend Lucy, who is a psychotherapist.

Hi Lucy,

Lovely to catch up with you yesterday – I forgot to ask you …
Recently I spoke to a funeral director – a friend of Charlotte's.
I wanted to ask him about 'what the dead wear'. I know – it's
a bit morbid but so much of the research I've been doing – about
fashion and life – includes death. Anyway, he said something
interesting that has been on my mind about how bereaved rela-
tives bring the clothes in for their loved ones – he said there is
often a strangeness, 'an awkwardness' about how they bring
them and give them to him. I just wondered if you may have
some thoughts on this.
XJ

Hi Jenny,
There's a phenomenon (originally identified by Freud) called
transference, where a client transfers onto their therapist the feel-
ings, expectations or attachment needs they have experienced in
early relationships, typically with a parent. Those transferred
feelings can be positive or negative, and usually become apparent
in behaviours. This could relate to how the bereaved bring in
their relative's clothes. You mentioned the funeral director
noticed there was sometimes an awkwardness. I associate awk-
wardness with embarrassment, discomfort, even shame, which
all suggest the presence of an 'other' – the deceased? The funeral
director? There could be a transference onto either, of historically

familiar emotions or expectations. Or the deceased might be the very person with whom those feelings or expectations originated.

For example – 'scrunched up in a bag, on a hanger, folded on their arm suggest they seem to have difficulty with the handling of them'. It all seems so full of symbolism: how we 'handle' death and things associated with it. Some can touch the clothes, perhaps they are able to connect with the full emotional force of death, the ultimate separation, while others perhaps can't face it, might need to keep things hidden in a bag.

Selecting the last clothes a loved one will ever wear is such an intimate and charged responsibility, a final act of how we show love and care for them. There's no chance of actual feedback and so we can only second-guess what the response would have been if the person were still alive. Those anticipated responses, including possible approval or disapproval for the choices we've made, would be based on the relationship dynamics with the living person, now transferred onto the deceased.

Ultimately, we all find our way towards different, creative, coping strategies in times of extreme emotion.

Lots of love xxx

Our relationship with the dead never rests. The communication becomes one-sided and unfair, spasmodic and unpredictable but, as time gently pulls the rug from beneath us, truths are revealed, ready to be dusted and dealt with, and the dialogue continues.

I read Lucy's email before I went to sleep and when I awoke the next morning, thoughts on the choosing my mother's clothes, the ones she would be buried in, were waiting for me. I recalled how the question of what I would like her to wear had shaken me and carelessly I had told my dad: 'Let's put her in the cotton thing.'

At the time, while I could manage the dot-to-dot arrangements of the funeral, my imagination had slipped away and my attempts at intuitive thinking had been piti-ful. But my reluctance to choose something from her wardrobe has always bothered me.

And then, nine years after my mother's death, I won-dered: had I been afraid of choosing the wrong thing, dressing her for eternity in something she wouldn't like? Such an unbearable thought, don't you think, to mess up on that last look?

In truth, nothing was ever quite right for my mum. There was always something slightly amiss with whatever I did. But somehow I always understood. I gathered early on that she had lost too much along the way to entertain the idea of lasting happiness, and so she would stymie it, turning off the party lights before anyone else could.

Unknowingly, she transferred her fears onto me, while simultaneously cushioning the blows with her immeasurable love, bestowing on me a confidence tinged with despair. I do regret not being brave enough to dress her, but I just couldn't risk it. Such are the thoughts on strange days.

You may be imagining that my mum was an elegant woman who followed the latest trends and drove up to London to buy from the designers' new collections – a woman who wore Manolos. So I feel I must put you right and give my mum the recognition she deserves. Rita was unique in both fashion sense and spirit. She had her own style, and it was often unexpected, out of place and mildly eccentric. My mum loved fashion and in particular her own version of it. Constantly reinventing herself, she would change up her style with some new fancy-rimmed glasses, a statement bag or a tartan wrap, and recolour her hair. And in my memories, I play, interchanging her accessories with her hair shades, never entirely sure if I've got the right combination. She never looked for an opinion or changed her mind; my mum wore whatever she wanted, wherever she wished, fighting fearlessly against suburban style, conventionality and dullness. Her braveness to experiment, to have a go and not give a damn, was my inspiration.

After all, what *is* the worst thing that can happen when you fuck up on the fashion front? Would a bomb drop on you?

So what will be my own epilogue? 'When I die, dress me in Jenny Packham!'

I'll design something special for the occasion. A beautiful dove-blue chiffon gown, fading to a pale ghostly grey at the hem as if dipped in dew. Draped delicately across the bodice will be gently pleated folds and from each shoulder I shall create trailing ties of silk that catch the breeze and fly up into the sky as I tread lightly across the clouds towards the bright white light, my ethereal style clinched by a rippling train flowing in my wake.

Please don't worry about creasing the material as you struggle to arrange the billowing skirts around me, or fret about my hair and make-up. I'm going for the natural look but, yes, I would look better with a smudge of my favourite lipstick. Perhaps I could wear a tiara, one with large pearly droplets and a veil of flimsy tulle. And remember, style me with very high, strappy, silvery slingbacks studded with a multitude of tiny crystals, which will sparkle incandescently as I step up onto the sweeping staircase, arriving at my very own After-Show Party. I am almost looking forward to this now! Finally, it is *my* time to shine.

But that was then.

A memoir can only ever be a slice of a life because, at the very moment you place the final full stop, time continues unpunctuated.

Shortly after completing my manuscript for this book, the luxury designer shops closed and weddings were postponed for a better, brighter day as the invisible enemy moved amongst us – coronavirus. Overnight fashion became inconsequential as our hearts and minds turned away from ourselves to others, sparkling gowns becoming irrelevant in the face of the desperate need for the practical Personal Protection Equipment.

We closed our studio, and from our kitchen table Mathew and I began to put together a plan to hibernate our company that designs and manufactures evening wear in a world that now just needed to stay home. After 32 years in the fashion industry the question of *how to make a dress* had never felt so troublesome.

But the time to celebrate and party will return – and I will dare to venture out again, leaving my 'lounge pants' crumpled on the bedroom floor, enthused to dress up once more.

So, rather than finish this book with a full stop, I will end it with an ellipsis …

Acknowledgements

I would like to thank the following people for their contribution towards this book:

Harriet Yates, Blaire Donald, Laura Rifkind, Anne St Lawrence, Simon Fowler, Tim O' Sullivan, Tamsin Ridgwell, Sarah Flawn, Rosemary Harden, David Downton, Zandra Rhodes, Magda Archer, Jon Gorrigan, Tom Jamieson, Lucy Berry, Adriana Candeias, Noa Karet, David Holmes, Richard Young, Ellen Von Unwerth, Albert Sanchez, Mario Testino, Tim Walker, Caterina Murino, and Dita Von Teese.

And then there are the others, my team: my husband Mathew for his gentle support and endless patience; my daughters, Georgia for always listening and Bern for her brutal, beautiful honesty; my friend Shirley Giles, who has been holding my hand since I was 6 years old; Charlotte Corney for her loving enthusiasm; my dad Colin for the stories and my brother Chris for letting me photograph his pants. I couldn't have done it without you.

I would also like to thank Andrew Goodfellow at Ebury Publishing for trusting in me, Claire Scott and Siofra Clancy for their work on the campaign, and Robyn Drury, my editor, for sculpting this book with passion and skill and for showing me how to make a book.

Between the lines there are others who may remember 'being there': I would like to thank you all for working with me and for adding colour to both these pages and my life.

Notes on Images

Page 1: My Jean Harlow-inspired mood board – a mixture of original photos and news clippings mixed with newer items, a lock of hair and lipstick-stained cigarettes. We were inspired by Jean's youthful personal wardrobe and her on screen 'bombshell' style.

Pages 2 and 3: A studio shot. The sewing machine was my grandmother Gertrude Smith's, and it was given to me when I was six years old. The dress to the left is 'Joy', which was inspired by a vintage dress found in the basement of a museum in Fort William that was embroidered with the wings of jewel beetles. This photograph is staged to look tidy – it's usually so much messier.

Pages 4 and 5: Dita's Carmen Miranda-inspired costume was our first collaboration. We created tropical flowers in satin and encrusted them with crystals, attaching them to a forties style design hand sewn with overlapping white sequins. At the end of her performance in LA, Dita was left wearing nothing but the thong and nipple pasties.

Pages 6 and 7: To celebrate the end of Dita's sell-out tour, I hosted a dinner for her and her friends at the Connaught hotel, and designed her dress for the event. The 'Lazy' costume [on page 7] has become one of Dita's most iconic looks. The wraparound gown covered in smokey blue sequins and crystals is trimmed with layers of hand curled feathers to create the dramatic sleeves.

Page 8: Women who capture our attention are often connoisseurs of colour. The Queen and Marilyn's love of colour (and diamonds) makes them both unforgettable.

Page 9: I have hundreds of these 'swatches'. They are embellishment ideas created to inspire the designs for a collection.

Pages 10 and 11: My favourite editorials by Tim Walker and Mario Testino.

Page 12: Photos of my family including my Dad, my brother Chris in his Gaultier coat, the infamous 'flamingo hat' and my Dad's jumper going up in flames.

Page 13: Mathew and my daughters Georgia and Bern; and Mum, Dad and Chris in the back garden.

Page 14: Kate Winslet looking resplendent on the red carpet for the Titanic 3D premiere at the Royal Albert Hall – the dress we made in 4 days.

Page 15: A few of the best red-carpet moments.

Page 16: Leo and me – the photo I was too ashamed to look at for months!

Page 17: Mathew and I in the Loggia Room at the Mandarin Oriental Hotel in London, December 2015 – taken just before we got married after 28 years together.

Page 18: I took this photograph at the Victoria and Albert Archive in Kensington. The dress belonged to Clara Mathews, who was married in 1880. Later I discovered she was the daughter of Isaac Merritt Singer – famous for producing the Singer sewing machine.

Page 19: My wedding dress was made from a dove blue Austrian lace, sewn together by hand without seams. My shoes were a gift from Christian Louboutin.

Page 20: A beautiful shot of our bridal gown 'Eden', photographed by the brilliant Ellen von Unwerth on location in France.

Page 21: Backstage images at our 'A Midsummer Night's Dream'-inspired bridal show in New York.

Page 22: This is a page dedicated to my friend, the artist Magda Archer – who invited me into both her wardrobe and studio.

Page 23: Chris Packham's pants. Shockingly showy and a reminder that you never know what lies beneath.

Page 24: Backstage images at the Linbury Studio Theatre. The show was inspired by the Ballet Russes and took inspiration from the sets and costumes from Diaghilev's productions. It was a beautiful show, but as the fake snow-flakes began to fall onto the catwalk, so did my mood as I suddenly realised – I had got it all wrong.

References

Every effort has been made to trace copyright holders and to obtain their permission for the use of copyright material. The publisher apologises for any errors or omissions in the above list and would be grateful if notified of any corrections that should be incorporated in future reprints or editions of this book.

All integrated images courtesy of Jenny Packham.

Endpaper photography by Jon Gorrigan.

Plate section images

Page 1: Jean Harlow collage photographed by Jon Gorrigan. All props courtesy of Jenny Packham.

Pages 2 and 3: Jenny Packham's office photographed by Jon Gorrigan.

Page 4: Sketches © Jenny Packham.

Page 5: Dita Von Teese collage photographed by Jon Gorrigan. Top photograph © Richard Young and bottom

Pages 16 and 17: Photographs courtesy of Jenny Packham.

Pages 18 and 19: Bridal outfits photographed by Jon Gorrigan.

Page 20: Photograph from Jenny Packham's SS11 bridal campaign, shot by Ellen von Unwerth and reproduced with kind permission of the photographer.

Page 21: Backstage bridal photography courtesy of Jenny Packham.

Page 22: Photographs of Magda Archer's wardrobe and personal items courtesy of Magda Archer. Magda Archer's artwork reproduced with kind permission of the artist. Photograph of Magda and Jenny © Jenny Packham. Spread photographed by Jon Gorrigan.

Page 23: Photograph of Chris Packham's underwear shot by Jon Gorrigan, with kind permission of Chris. Photograph of Chris with jumper © Chris Packham.

Page 24: Backstage photography courtesy of Jenny Packham.